This is a work of non-fiction. In most instances, names, locations, and other identifying details have been changed to protect individual privacy.

ISBN: 978-0-578-91865-5

Library of Congress Control Number: 2021910210

Author Photograph by Catalyst Photography
Architectural Illustration by Michael Nguyen
Book Cover by Elements & Ink Media, LLC
Book Illustrations by Elements & Ink Media, LLC

I Should Have Wrote A Book

Extraordinary Tales from Ordinary People

Thomas Person

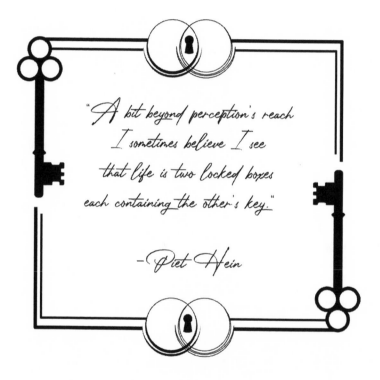

"A bit beyond perception's reach
I sometimes believe I see
that life is two locked boxes
each containing the other's key."

-Piet Hein

ACKNOWLEDGMENTS

Thanks to:

First and foremost, my mother. Where do I even begin? You were my everything, and you left far too soon. I am proud to have grown up with someone like you as my guide and my leader, showing me how to navigate this complicated experience we call life. I will be forever grateful to you for everything you taught me and passed on to me. I am who I am today, because of you. This book is for you. I love you, and I miss you.

My Nano for being an inspiration to so many including me. Writing this book was one of the hardest things I have ever done, but you taught me that hard work is truly rewarding. Your life was the origin story for this book, and it was your words that started everything in motion.

Nick, my editor at Gold Medal Editing. You managed to guide me through this process and bring my writing to a level I didn't think was possible.

Everyone who has a story featured in this book, thank you for sitting with me and allowing me to tell your story in the best way possible. You put up with me badgering you with endless questions. Your patience is genuinely appreciated.

All of my friends, family, and loved ones who were in the know on this secret little project of mine. Whether it was reading early drafts and giving feedback, helping me put pieces of these stories together, or having the difficult conversations with me when I was being stubborn, I am eternally grateful. I am so lucky to be surrounded by people who continue to amaze and inspire me. All of the joy and sorrow we have shared as friends and family was poured into every sentence of this book to give it life.

TABLE OF CONTENTS

The Important

The Unbelievable

The Gritty

The Ugly

The Ridiculous

INTRODUCING:
I SHOULD HAVE WROTE A BOOK

arely have we had the chance to pay tribute to the tales told around the campfire, or the stories shared at the dinner table. These are the types of stories that have become an intimate part of us, shared with those closest to us countless times, because we continue to enjoy them no matter how many times we hear or tell them. This book features 13 incredible stories intended to shine the spotlight on the moments in our lives that have had a lasting impact, allowing them to take their final bow in front of an audience and get the recognition they deserve.

While some of these stories are my own, others belong to those closest to me, such as family members or people I might as well call family. In every case, some details are being changed to protect identities and maintain the privacy of everyone being featured. I spoke with every single person featured in this book and got permission to use their story. Simply put, without them, this book doesn't exist. They shall be the narrators, and this book will be the medium to give the best possible representation of the story they love to tell in all its glory.

Like all stories passed down from generation to generation, I operate under the assumption that much like any fishing story, these may have been exaggerated, and this is the form they shall maintain in this book, embellishment and all. With this in mind, I gave each narrator a chance to reflect on their experience after telling their story. It gives them the chance to look back on the events that occurred and discuss how this experience did or didn't affect them in the long term. It gives a unique opportunity to hear how they feel about their story now that years, or in some cases decades, have passed.

Now, one thing most people know about me is that I am obsessively organized. I love few things more than crossing an item off my checklist or organizing a bin and putting everything contained in its place. So, to add that little bit of my character to this book, I have taken the time when weaving all these stories together to classify them. These categories are The Important, The Unbelievable, The Gritty, The Ugly, and The Ridiculous. I did this to help give a feel for what someone is about to experience when reading each story. A pre-framing if you will. Since each chapter is its own standalone story and is not tied to the other, I felt it was important to set a tone of sorts.

Typically, when someone goes to a bookstore or surfs the internet for a new book to read, they search for a specific type of book they are interested in. We all know the internet has an endless array of best "insert genre here" novels of the year lists so that avid readers can get their fill of what they desire. However, this book doesn't really follow the rules in any standard way. A grouping of short, unrelated stories can be anything they want to be, so classifying this book under a single umbrella term is a bit difficult, which is why I did it for you. You're welcome.

The Important

The important is just that; it's important. If you're reading this sentence right now, you've already made it here. The section helps you gain an understanding of the mission the book seeks to accomplish, and in the next chapter, I explain the deeper, more personal inspiration behind my desire to write the very words you are currently reading. The important is short, sweet, and to the point, but it is necessary to read in order to get the full effect of the book.

The Unbelievable

I truly believe each story told in this book actually happened, but this section will definitely make you question this. Sometimes we experience things we just can't explain, and they seem so impossible, that it makes it hard to believe the person telling the story. That is why this category is called the unbelievable.

I am an incredibly skeptical person by nature. My friends will tell you as much and often fault me for being this way, but I can't help it. Part of my skeptical process starts by asking a few simple questions. Why would someone stick their neck out and risk being called crazy for telling this kind of story and what, if anything, is in it for them? Keep in mind, each of the stories in this book has been told by people I know very well or by yours truly. They do not have a reason to lie and if you question them, they will swear on their own life the validity of their statements. I have often tried to find reasonable explanations for the things these people experienced, and in some cases I do. However, I have left my own opinion out of this and instead, I leave it to you, the reader, as to whether you walk away convinced or truly find these unbelievable.

The Gritty

Here we have all the stories about persevering through difficult times or situations. They are about determination and choosing to attack the situation you're confronted with head-on, rather than run away. I often find these types of stories to be the most inspiring. When faced with overwhelming odds stacked against them, the characters in these stories put their heads down and charged forward at all costs. They are the heroes of their story. The ones who made it out when no one else could. It takes guts and it takes grit to go through and do what they have done.

The Ugly

I want to give an honest warning about the ugly because these stories are not for the faint of heart. This is also not some melodramatic warning. I genuinely mean this. These stories hold a special, yet terrible place in the minds of the people who have experienced them. These stories are true and to tell them properly meant not holding back. Doing so would be a disservice to them.

Consider this the rated R section of the book, since it deals with heavier topics such as violence, abuse, gore, and even death. These are the stories that people kept inside, bearing the weight they weren't willing to share with others until now. Read at your own risk.

The Ridiculous

It's always best to end on a lighter note, right? Some stories don't really contain a lesson to learn, and they don't really serve a purpose other than being a fun tale to tell. These are the stories that are often told at someone's expense. They are usually embarrassing or so ludicrous that they may even walk a fine line between this section and The Unbelievable. But, when everything is said and done, they are indeed, just ridiculous.

Enjoy!

MY INSPIRATION

When my mother passed away, it opened up a world of things I didn't know about her. I spent so much time sitting at the kitchen table in the home where I grew up, flipping through old photo albums that I have never seen before. Honestly, it amazed me how much traveling she did when she was younger. I travel quite a bit myself, and I was astounded to see how many of the same places we had been to. It was another connection that I could hold onto since her passing.

I soon found out that the pictures were really just the tip of the iceberg. There were stories about her, told through family and friends, that I had never heard before, maybe for good reason. At what point would she find it important to tell me about the time she basically did the splits between a boat and the dock before falling into the water? Maybe she was too shy to ever tell me about how she was a runner-up for a city-wide beauty pageant when she was younger. It made me realize that as people gathered around to share their memories of my mother, both good and bad, that I had a very limited understanding of who she really was. To put it simply, my mom was just that to me, my mom. I never gave her an existence beyond that self-imposed boundary. Sure, she raised me and took care of me. She was one of the kindest people I've ever known. But somehow, through the years, I never stopped to think about my mom outside of my own narrow lens. Who was this person that raised me? What was she like when she was my age? What were her inner thoughts, her dreams, and aspirations? What were the stories and secrets she only shared with the people closest to her? Sadly, these are things I may never know.

I came to a sudden realization. Listening to the stories we tell each other gives a glimpse into who we are. It helps us understand one another. We can learn so much about someone else by listening to their stories. It gives insight into their personalities and helps us create a more complete picture of how we can relate to one another. We are made of moments, combined over time to make the story that is our life.

As I dug deeper into finding out who my mother really was, it led me to have a conversation with my dad. As we took a drive down memory lane, somehow, we ended up talking about my great grandfather or as I knew him, my Nano. It is widely known in my family that he lived a pretty incredible life filled with many ups and downs. He didn't talk about it all that much, because mind you, the life he lived was not by choice, it was by circumstance. He was an Italian immigrant, and his trip to the United States wasn't exactly the standard run-of-the-mill coming to America for opportunity story that we all too often hear. It would be better classified under a harrowing escape from a life he didn't want to live.

Fast-forward another 60 plus years and you would see my dad speaking to my Nano during his final days. He knew his time was coming, as is everyone's. He even told my father that he was ready to die, and it was in that moment that my dad asked a very pointed question to a man he respected immensely. "Was it a good life?"

After a long and thoughtful pause, my Nano looked back at him, eyes withered and tired, cheeks sunken in from lack of appetite, and said, "You know Dave, I should have wrote a book."

It is this conversation, this one statement, that was the driving force behind my desire to write this book. We all have people like my Nano or my mother in our lives. They are seemingly ordinary people, walking among us that have lived incredible lives, or at the very least have some pretty incredible stories to tell. After all, the people we often focus on reading about are the true game changers in our society, and rightfully so. However, the intention of this book is different. It is meant to highlight those moments in our lives that stand out. This is about the story you can't wait to tell your friends, or maybe it's the one story that's always been too hard to share. It is the good, the bad, and the great. It is the unbelievable, the extraordinary, and the ugly. It features the tales we tell to our loved ones about the things we believe only they will care about. But in truth, these stories, whether happy or sad, enlightening or funny, joyful or serious, deserve the spotlight for all to hear.

PSYCHIC FOR A DAY

<u>Frank</u>

I was 19 years old, and I was finally about to take a big step into the real world of working. I had just been accepted into an ironworker's apprenticeship, which was due to begin in just a little more than 2 weeks. My friend and roommate at the time, Mike, had been accepted into the same apprenticeship and as we sat around one day, it struck us that all our free time and our ability to do whatever we wanted, whenever we wanted, was about to go away. So, we made a plan to go down swinging into the real world. Our goal was a very ambitious one, probably too ambitious, but we were young, dumb, full of energy, and ready to take on the world.

We lived in Illinois at the time, but I had family in California and Arizona, and Mike had family in the Dakotas. We made the decision to go on a two-week-long road trip that would start by going straight to California, down to Arizona, back up through the Dakotas, and then home, all within two weeks. 7,000 miles in two weeks. If that sounds insane, it's because it is.

The trip started off fine and the first part of the drive, although a very long one, was uneventful. We made it to California just fine and spent plenty of time visiting our family and friends when we could. There was one small hiccup when we went down into Tijuana. We got stopped at the border as we were coming back through customs and got strip-searched. To be fair, we did look like a bunch of hippies at the time. I was about 5'8" with long blonde hair and a pretty good-sized beard. Mike was a tall guy, well over 6 ft with long black hair and a huge black beard. We were both in shape from our line of work, so we admittedly fit the profile of well-built hippie drug smugglers. Thankfully, we had nothing on us other than some souvenirs and they let us go.

We continued to hang out with family during the days and drove during the nights. It was incredibly unsafe to be running on as little sleep as we were, but it was the only way to make our ridiculous timeline work. Arizona came and went with no problems at all, allowing us to begin the final leg of our journey up to the Dakota's.

Upon arrival to see Mike's family, we were running pretty low on energy. When visiting, we did our best to be as alert as possible, but they definitely got the short end of the stick. We had either been driving for long hours, spending time with family for long hours, or partying with family and friends for long hours. The only thing we had not been doing for long hours was sleeping. So, with our body's batteries running dangerously low, we decided to leave and head back home while we could still function at all. We had somehow managed to accomplish everything we had set out to do at the beginning of our trip. If I tried to do something like this today, it would literally kill me.

The drive was agonizingly difficult as we fought to keep our eyes open. We were driving through an area near Keystone, South Dakota, and had just visited Mount Rushmore not long before. We were doing our best to maintain our excitement over the chance to drive through the Badlands National Park next. It was the part of the drive I was looking forward to the most. However, my brain was having none of it. The car was acting like a cradle, rocking side to side with the winding roads putting me to sleep. After Mike nearly dozed off at the wheel several times, we decided to stop and get a late breakfast while we recharged.

As we discussed our options on where to stop something hit me. My body felt weighed down by what I can only describe as a presence. It felt as though something was trying to consume my mind and my thoughts. I shook my head a little trying to clear my thoughts, thinking maybe we had one too many sleepless nights and my body was beginning to revolt. I wasn't sure if I was going to get sick or what, but I had never felt like this before. This is going to sound a little crazy, but as we drove along, I began to experience reality differently. Everything began to feel like DeJa'Vu. Like I had done this before and been here before. Even crazier, I swear I knew what would happen next. It felt like I was watching a movie I had already seen or was reading a book that I have read many times. My surroundings took on a sense of familiarity. The areas on the side of the road felt familiar in the same way pulling onto your street going home might feel familiar to you. You might see the white picket fence and know that means your house is just ahead on the left. I had that very same feeling looking at rocks and markers on the road; like I was going home or at least to somewhere I had been many times before.

"How about here?" I could hear Mike's voice like a distant echo in the background.

"Hey! Frank!" Mike raised his voice and waved his hand in front of my face to snap me out of it.

"Yeah. Here is fine. Sorry."

"You okay?" Mike asked.

"Yeah. Yeah. Just tired, I think. Sorry. I'm fine."

I wasn't fine. My mind was racing trying to discern what this feeling was as we pulled into the parking lot of an old diner. It was a decent sized building, but old with what seemed like a lot of the original wood. It was exactly what one would expect an old-timey diner in the upper Midwest to be. Basically, it was like what a Cracker Barrell is trying to imitate, just minus all the nicer things one would get at a modern restaurant. As we went up the few steps leading to the front door and entered the restaurant, I felt uneasy.

The inside of the restaurant was all wood to match like the outside. Walls on either side had booths, with tables taking all the space in between, and in the middle of everything was a round bar area with people already bellied-up starting their drinking for the day despite it being just after 10am. You could hear the murmur of many different conversations happening all at once, since many of the folks that come to places like this do so almost every day as part of their routine, meeting with friends or family each day.

We were quickly seated at our table, and I still couldn't shake the feeling. The more I fought it, the more it dug its roots in and pushed back. Thankfully, at least at this point in my life, I was a pretty laid-back guy. I was good at not letting things bother me too much and going with the flow. So, I took a deep breath, sat back in my chair, and let whatever this was take its course.

Immediately, my body felt heavy again, both physically and emotionally. Now, for what came next, I have tried explaining a million times to a million people what this feeling was like but putting it into words has always been difficult. I started to see flashes of the events in my mind. Somehow, I was aware that these events hadn't happened yet. The flashes came from different perspectives than my own. I would get to see and hear conversations at the table next to us that hadn't yet occurred in the present. I knew what vehicles were going to pull into the parking lot next. It was like accessing a memory and watching it play in my mind, despite that memory existing in the future. Unfortunately, I had no control over when it was happening and what I was able to see. It just came and went as it pleased. The easiest way to describe it is a psychic ability, but it wasn't like I could just read minds or something. It was more complex. I felt as though I was experiencing two different realities at the same time. I was both present in the moment as myself, and experiencing what I believe to be the future at the same time.

This was getting a bit too weird, even for my calm nature.

"Mike, this might sound a bit odd, but I think I can see the future right now."

Mike lurched forward coughing like he was trying not to spit a drink out, despite not having anything yet. He took a moment to look me over.

"I knew something was up with you. I think we need some more sleep, my friend." he chuckled through his words, clearly not believing a single word I just said. I can't really blame him, honestly.

"I'm serious. I don't know what is happening, but I swear I can see the future or something right now. It started happening just before we got here." I insisted and pleaded with him that I wasn't kidding around. That's when it struck me. Another flash came to me and I knew what was going to happen next. I took a look around the table to confirm that everything was the same as the vision I had just received. "Okay, Frank. Maybe we shou…." I cut Mike off in the middle of his sentence. There was no time. I knew if I did something more drastic, maybe I could convince him that my newly gained powers were real.

"Mike, it's difficult to get to the bathroom from where we are sitting because they are renovating right now. You have to walk all the way down to the other end, go to the right, and head through the hall. Then you have to walk through a separate dining area before making a left and it is at the back of that hallway. Men's is the second door on the right, but you can just ask another waitress if you get lost. They would understand and you wouldn't be the first to ask."

Mike looked at me a bit shocked and kind of pissed off that I had rudely cut him off but said, "Good, I need to use the bathroom anyway? Man, you sure are acting weird. You been here before?" "No" I replied, "But that's what you are going to ask and that is almost word for word how she is going to reply."

"She?" Mike said, tilting his head like a confused puppy.

"Good morning," the waitress said as she arrived at our table. "What can I get you gentlemen started with this morning?"

Mike snapped his head quickly and turned to her, still looking a bit confused by my actions. "Ummmmmm...." he took another moment to clear his throat. "Yeah, uhhh, good morning. Tell you what, I think we both need a minute still, but can we get started with waters?" he asked.

"Oh, of course. No problem at all. Anything else?" the waitress kindly asked.

Mike paused for a moment, probably wondering internally if he should say the next part or not. I could see him look at me out of the corner of his eye.

"Also, where is the restroom located?" he asked.

"Oh, it's a good thing you asked because it is a bit difficult to get to the bathroom from this area of the restaurant due to the renovations. You have to walk all the way down to the other end, go to the right, and head through the hall. Then you have to walk through a separate dining area before making a left and it is at the back of that hallway. Men's is the second door on the right, but you can just ask another waitress if you get lost. They would understand and you wouldn't be the first to ask."

"Thank you." Mike said to the waitress as she turned to walk away while he slowly turned to me and said, "What the fuck, Frank? How did you do that? Are you messing with me?"

His tone had changed. I had his attention now.

"I told you. I'm dead serious. Now, I'll tell you more when you get back from the bathroom."

I waited patiently for Mike to return to the table while I made my best attempt at focusing on my newly acquired abilities. The flashes continued to come and go as they pleased, but the feeling that accompanied them still felt the same. It was a heavy presence just weighing on me. I managed to stay calm despite this unrecognizable feeling as a few more minutes passed, and Mike returned to the table. He sat down, leaned back in his chair with his arms folded and a stern look on his face, clearly thinking about what to say next as we sat in silence for a few moments. He leaned forward, placing his forearms on the table and clasping his hands together as he cocked his head to the side a bit looking at me in utter disbelief.

"Bullshit." He said harshly. "Total bullshit."

He still thought I was messing with him. "Mike, I swear I'm not screwing around here. This is just as weird to me as it probably is to you. You have to believe me." I pleaded my case.

"I don't have to believe shit. Let's just drop it, okay?"

He wasn't going to believe me yet, but I knew Mike better than anyone. I could tell he was questioning it. I could see the wheels spinning and the gears turning in his head as the waitress came back to the table and we ordered our food. He would come around.

We enjoyed a nice big meal and just before we were getting up to leave Mike leaned back into the table. "Explain it to me one more time and is whatever this is, still happening?" Mike asked calmly.

"Yeah, it's been happening this whole time. Honestly, it's hard to explain, but just before we pulled up to the restaurant, I started not feeling well. Then, I started hallucinating, or so I thought, but everything I was seeing happened a few moments later. I could see the future. I can still see the future. And yes, I know how crazy that sounds." I explain to him one more time as well as I could. Mike, looked at me, squinting his eyes really trying to study me to see if I was lying.

"Okay. I'm not sure what exactly is going on here, but I don't think you're lying. I just don't think you can see the future, Frank. Let's get out of here. I'm driving and you should try to get some sleep."

I was slowly getting him on my side. We paid our bill and went to leave the restaurant, but as we walked out the door and towards the car, I felt uneasy again. The presence in my body started to feel even heavier than before. It shifted and changed in nature as images of a lone buffalo, staring at me while standing off the road on top of a ridge passed before my eyes. In between images of the buffalo came roads, signs, and other landmarks. As each image flashed through my mind it came with an intense urge or need, to see this buffalo. I started to feel anxious again as the images passed. It reminded me of being back in school and having a big project due that I had been procrastinating on. It felt like something bad could happen if I didn't complete the task being assigned to me. In other words, it felt like something was questing me to see this lone buffalo, but I couldn't understand why.

I turned to Mike, "How do you feel about making a side trip?" he looked at me, completely disinterested. "Mike, I'm getting more images. There is a buffalo out there somewhere and I feel like the reason I'm seeing these images is because of this buffalo. We need to go find it so I can figure out why this is happening. Please."

As expected, he looked at me like I was completely crazy. "That's the exact opposite of getting some sleep but screw it. Let's do it."

He was finally on board. We got in the car and he pulled out a map, asking me to point to where we needed to go.

"We won't be needing a map," I said. "I'm not sure where it is exactly but I keep seeing landmarks or signs that I think are leading the way. We will know how to get there as we go. I just know."

I pointed in a random direction based purely on instinct and off we went. Chills began to run through my body and flashes would pass through my mind leading us in the direction we needed to go next. Neither of us had any idea where we were or where we were actually going, only that a lone buffalo was waiting for us at our final destination. Since I had never been to this part of South Dakota in my life, the best I could do to help lead Mike where to go, was to close my eyes allowing each image to flash in my mind. I would take a moment to explore them, like looking at all the finer details of a painting, to pick out landmarks, which would indicate where we should go next.

As we went over hills and through rural small towns in the middle of nowhere, I started to get the hang of it.

"Alright. Drive on this road for a bit longer and we will come to a T in the road. I can see an old man, driving a beat-up white pickup truck with a dog in the bed of the truck. We need to turn left there."

We drove along and wouldn't you know it, we came to the T in the road, with the old man and his dog exactly like I said. The old man stared at us, mostly because Mike was staring at him awkwardly, still in disbelief of what was happening.

Now Mike was all in. "Frank, this is insane. What is happening right now? Where do we go next?" Mike said basically bouncing up and down in the driver's seat, anxiously awaiting my next command. Sometimes we both would even start to get worried when we drove for long stretches with no visions coming to me. We had no idea where we were and even if we stopped now, figuring out where we were wasn't going to be easy. I remember hoping that these visions came with return directions because as much as I could sense we were heading in the right direction, we were also very lost.

The roads began to get more and more narrow as we drove further into the backcountry of these rural areas. It was past mid-day now and the sun was beating down, shining brightly off the winding, long, and very hilly roads as we looked off to the plains on both sides of us. Some hills were steep enough to the point that you couldn't see what is past each one until you crest it.

"Oh, you've got to be kidding me," I said, snapping out of the long streak with no visions. "What? What is it now?" Mike answered back, with excitement in his voice.

"Slow down a bit. Once we get over the hill, there is going to be a station wagon on the side of the road. There will be a family with three kids and a mule is going to have its head inside the window as all of them are freaking out."

"Get out of here," Mike responded in disbelief, even though he took my advice and started to slow down.

We came to the top of the hill and sure enough, after we crested to the other side, there it was. A station wagon with two parents and three kids, all in a complete panic because of the mule that was sticking its head through the back-passenger side window. We figured they must have pulled over to look at it and as it got closer to them, they stupidly offered it food. A regrettable decision now since it clearly didn't go as planned. I've never cleaned up mule drool before, but I'm sure it is about as pleasant as it sounds.

As we passed the family by, it quickly ended the dry spell of no visions. I started to feel this presence in me grow stronger, like a magnet drawn to metal, I could feel the pull getting stronger. Images came and went. I continued giving more directions such as turning at broken fences or using certain parts of the road to indicate where we needed to go next. We had been driving without a map into unknown areas for nearly 2 hours at this point. We were close and I knew it. I could feel my heart beating, building with anticipation, knowing we were going to find the buffalo. I would fulfill this quest that had been given to me. I had no idea what was going to happen when we did, but I knew this was what I was supposed to do.

I leaned forward in the vehicle, putting my hand on the dash. I rolled down the window, letting in the warm summer's day air, and stuck my head slightly out the window to confirm my thoughts. I could feel it. "Up here. Just over the hill. It's there." I said to Mike. I knew it was there. I knew it was there in the very same way that you are certain you know where you are at this very moment. It was a sense of certainty I have rarely felt before.

We crested the hill and started to slow down. We were met by the sun shining brightly, illuminating an absolutely massive buffalo standing just to the right of us on the side of the road. This was it. It was him. This is what we have been searching for. The buffalo stared at us, making a few grunting and bellowing noises, occasionally dipping his head down to graze as we sat there and watched. It was just as I had seen it in my visions.

We had arrived at the end of our quest. I closed my eyes, waiting for more visions, more flashes to come and tell me what to expect next, but there was nothing. Mike stayed completely quiet, trying to give me the space needed to be as accommodating as possible. I tried to relax and free my mind, allowing thoughts to come and go as they pleased, but that was all that came or went. The visions had stopped, and I didn't know why.

Don't get me wrong, I didn't expect the buffalo to look up at us and start explaining to us the mysteries of life or anything. However, it did feel like something was missing. Like arriving at the door to the secret room and not having the key to see what was inside. I was waiting for a sense of completion that never really came. I wasn't sure if we completed our journey or if we had missed our chance, but sadly, deep down, I knew that nothing more was going to happen. I was just having a hard time accepting it. We had spent so much time seeking out this buffalo and it felt like it was all for nothing in the end.

I looked back to the buffalo, standing there, unmoving and stoic, mouth opening and closing as he chewed on the grass beneath his hooves.

"We can go whenever you're ready," I told Mike.

"Wait, so that's it? Huh. I thought there would be something more." He replied, clearly feeling the same sense of incompleteness that I was going through.

"Yeah…….me too. Let's go home and try to get some sleep."

"Copy that!" Mike said enthusiastically.

He pulled out a map to figure out where in the hell we were as he took off and started driving. As we went along the road, I watched in the side view mirror as the lone buffalo got smaller and smaller until we crested the next hill and he disappeared from view.

Suddenly, a chill ran through my body in a way I had never felt before in my life. It was the presence I had been feeling all day. It was like it manifested itself into my very being, desperately trying to separate itself from me. All the heaviness and weight I had been feeling the whole day, started to dissipate. I began instead to feel like I was floating, both literally and figuratively relieved of a burden that I had been carrying with me the entire time. I took a deep breath and let my eyes shut ever so slowly, allowing myself to completely relax as it gradually dispersed, leaving my body, escaping through every pore. That was it. It was gone and it wasn't coming back. I just knew.

"It's over," I said calmly to Mike

"Really? How do you know?" he asked.

"I can't explain it. It just left. It's gone."

"It?" he asked.

"Yeah…….it."

The rest of the drive was thankfully uneventful. We had had enough excitement to last us for a bit. After the presence left me, I remember feeling a bit sad for a little while. I oddly wanted more from what had occurred. It was like some unanswered riddle and I know I was close to solving it, but I missed my chance. But life goes on and as I said before, I was never the type to let things bother me or keep me down for long.

When we returned, I told a few people about what had happened and before they could all call me a liar, Mike would eagerly jump in and defend me to the very end. It was nice to know that because he was there, he believed me and believed in what happened. It usually resulted in everyone walking away thinking both of us were a bit insane and we felt it was best if we never really talk about it again with others. It would be our secret. Our story to tell.

Now, it has been decades since it originally occurred, and I don't feel as shy about telling this story. I know what happened and Mike knew what happened, but ironically enough, I'm not sure anyone will ever truly know what happened that day.

Reflection

This trip came as a last hurrah before the apprenticeship that I ended up leaving not long after it started anyway, but that is a different story altogether.

This entire experience, whatever it was, has no good explanation. Trust me. Once the internet was invented, I did my fair share of searching. Whatever this was, not even the internet has good answers, although WebMD says I'm probably dying of something or other. Typical.

After this occurred, I wasn't really sure what to think. Honestly, I kind of kept waiting for it to come back. The thought ran through my head that maybe I had some sort of gift. I don't claim to understand any of what happened, but that's the most sense I could make of it. I have always thought that spirits are possibly real and maybe they can attach themselves to me more easily than others. I'm not really sure since saying that out loud sounds a bit crazy. But then again, the entire experience was crazy so I might as well stick with a theme I guess, and it is also important to note that I'm not making a living in the circus predicting the future, so clearly my gifts were temporary at best. Either way, the entire idea of this trip was nuts and this experience was just icing on the cake.

I don't know why we needed to see that buffalo. All I know is it felt like a quest that we needed to complete. Everything that I predicted in between or had visions of, were just bonuses. They were simply confirmation that I was on to something and we were headed in the right direction. I have often wondered if maybe whatever presence took a hold of me that day, has some sort of special connection to the buffalo. I wonder if my experience has been shared by others, maybe even in the same area. Who knows? Regardless, I am happy this happened to me because it has given me a wonderfully weird and thought-provoking story to share for all to enjoy.

MAN ON THE TRAIN

<u>Robert</u>

I was on an adventure, backpacking throughout Japan over the course of a few weeks. I had nothing but the limited supplies in my forty-liter backpack. I had been to the country many times before, but I had never taken a trip like this. Typically, I stuck to a route known as the golden route, which consisted of Tokyo, Kyoto, and Hiroshima. This time, however, I would be going from location to location, heading out into the countryside and seeing everything it had to offer outside of the giant cities Japan is typically known for.

Taking this trip was like living a dream. I had wanted to do this for years, but it couldn't have come at a worse time for me. I had so many things going on in my life that all seemed to hit me at once. My mother's health was failing as my long-term relationship had recently fallen apart, while taking on the strain of multiple college degrees all at once, and on top of this, I was dealing with the passing of my Grandma, which resulted in my family basically erupting into a greed-driven civil war over inheritance, which I got planted firmly in the middle of. This was the first time in years that I had time to breathe and think about the toll everything had been taking on me. At the time, I should have been happy, setting off on an adventure that I had only dreamed about to this point, but instead, I was immensely sad. For the first time in years, I was doing something I wanted to do, and I was supposed to be leaving all the stress of the real world behind me temporarily. However, an unexpected side-effect of this trip seemed to be that I had too much time to think. I was traveling alone, so there was no one to keep me company. It was just me and my thoughts. I began to finally feel all the effects of the stress I had accumulated over the years. I was like a pot, ready to boil over at any minute and unfortunately, this trip ended up being the catalyst for that to happen.

In the middle of my backpacking adventure, I decided to take a quick, two-day long side trip to one of my favorite places to visit in Japan. The name of the town I visited was Nara. It isn't a very big city by Japan's standards with a population of around 350,000. There are plenty of tourists and tourism, so it wasn't exactly in line with the remainder of the trip in the countryside, but despite being an attraction for foreigners and natives alike, it still somehow feels like you've escaped far away from the hustle and bustle of the bigger cities when you're there.

There are 2 things most people visit Nara for. First and foremost are the roaming deer. There are about 1,200 of them throughout the city, mostly packed into Nara Park. They are considered sacred by the town and are protected. Although they are still wild animals, they have gotten very used to humans and walk around hoping that someone will feed them the wafers that many of the vendors surrounding the park sell for that very reason. If you come across them and they aren't being overly aggressive for the food, some of the deer even bow their head slightly to ask for food. Bowing is obviously a huge tradition in Japanese culture, but I've never really looked up if this was a purposely conditioned practice shown to the animals, or if it is something they just picked up on. Either way, it's a fun little highlight to experience during any trip.

The second reason people go, and specifically why I love going, is Todaiji Temple. It is an absolutely huge, incredibly beautiful temple, and inside of it stands a 150-foot-tall bronze Buddha statue, which is one of the three great Buddha's in Japan. Each time I make it to Japan for any reason, a trip to Nara is always on my to-do list.

After trying to enjoy my final night in the town, I watched as the sun began poking through the windows while lying on the tatami mats in my AirBnB room that I had rented for the night. I didn't get much sleep. My mind was glued to the negative thoughts that had been following me since day one of this entire trip. I needed to get an early start, so I gathered what little belongings I was carrying with me and headed out the door into what was supposed to be a beautiful summer Saturday. The air was crisp and cool for the morning, just the type of thing that should make you want to take a deep breath and move forward into your day with a sense of purpose and direction. Normally I would feel refreshed and energetic, but sadly, I didn't have the same sense of joy or rejuvenation that typically coincides with my visits to

Nara. Honestly, I was completely deflated and depressed. I couldn't shake all these thoughts in my head. I dragged my feet as I walked to the train station, intending to catch one of the early morning trains heading out of town.

Once I arrived at the station, I quickly bought my ticket and was one of the first people boarding the train heading back to Kyoto, which would act as my next launching pad into a different part of the countryside down south. Thankfully, this train was a semi-rapid, meaning it makes fewer stops than the local trains, but the ride was still going to be at least an hour or so.

I walked through the two sliding doors onto the train looking around as the sun shown on the bright red seats, which sit 2 people per row with an aisle down the middle, much like a school bus does. However, something stood out as odd to me. These seats faced one another on each side of the train. One seat faced towards the front and one seat faced towards the back, forcing you to look directly at the people sitting only a few feet in front of you. This could make things a bit awkward because in Japanese culture, staring or direct eye contact is seen as rude. It more or less forced you to sit there and play on your phone or just stare at the ground.

As I put my headphones into my ears, turning on my relaxation music mix, I walked about two-thirds of the way to the end of the nearly empty train car until I found a spot far enough away and sat down at a window seat, facing empty seats that no one had taken yet. Thankfully, with it being an early morning train on the weekend, not many people were traveling yet, so I wasn't too concerned with awkward interactions. That is until we came to the 2nd or 3rd stop about 20 minutes into the ride when an elderly Japanese man walked through the doors. He took a few steps in through the sliding doors and just stood there as the doors shut behind him. He was wearing loosely fitting, white clothing with a tan unzipped windbreaker and a tan paddy cap, which had grey hair peeking out from its edges. His face was spotted with darker areas and even through the slight smile on his face, he looked pretty worn down and tired. He waited a moment before carefully scanning the train car looking for which of the many empty seats he would decide to occupy. I watched him as he stood there making his mind up until he spotted me, sitting kind of slouched over, head pressed against the window of the train. I put my head down, although I could feel his gaze still locked onto me. I carefully tilted my head up, trying not to make any more awkward eye contact. I didn't want to give off the impression that I was looking for company.

The train had begun moving as I peeked upwards, catching a glimpse of him walking in my direction. I noticed he used a cane in one hand while the other grabbed onto the tops of seats to stabilize himself as he slowly moved forward, little by little, cautiously planning each of his steps to make sure any sudden movements of the train wouldn't knock him off balance. The train continued picking up speed as he continued bypassing all the empty seats, eventually making it to where I was sitting. He stood there for another moment whilst I did my best job to look out the window, watching the countryside come into view under the bright blue cloudless sky and pretend like I hadn't noticed him until he took a deep breath and sat down in the seat directly facing my own.

I wanted nothing to do with this. In fact, I was rather annoyed and considered getting up and moving to a different spot. If staring wasn't already considered rude, I would have made it a point to look up and give him the evil eye for having disturbed my solitude. I feel like my demeanor should have made it pretty clear that I wasn't interested in company. Read the room for Christ's sake. I just wanted to be alone and deal with all the things going on in my head.

"Good morning."

"You have got to be kidding me," I thought to myself. Now he's going to talk to me? Since my headphones were still in, the thought crossed my mind to act like I didn't hear anything and just ignore him. However, he was persistent.

"Hello! Good morning!" he said again as he waved his hand gently in front of my face from a distance, trying to get my attention. I slowly raised my head up, removing it from the window. I looked at him out of the corner of my eye, slowly and methodically removing my headphones to convey my annoyance with his bothersome actions.

"Where you from?" he asked. His English was very good, which caught my attention because it's not common in rural Japan.

"Chicago," I responded, even though I'm technically not from Chicago, but this is what I always told people when they asked since it was close enough.

"Ahhhhhhh Chicago! The windy city!" he exclaimed. "So cold all the time."

At this point, I decided to put my headphones that were currently still in my hand away completely since there was clearly no escaping this conversation anymore. It didn't matter how much I didn't want to talk. He seemed so nice, and I didn't have it in me to be rude to him no matter how bad my day was going.

"During the winter, it is very cold, but the summer can be very warm too," I informed him. He seemed very surprised by this, apparently thinking that Chicago must just be a frozen tundra all the time. He temporarily discontinued his questioning as he nodded his head, occasionally looking up almost like he was trying to process the mind-blowing information I had just given him about the general climate of Northern Illinois. After a few more moments of this, he brought his hand to his face, cupping his chin, and began stroking his cheeks the same way someone would stroke their beard if he had one. He turned his gaze down from the ceiling of the train and set it straight on me instead. His eyes suddenly had an intensity that previously wasn't there. His entire presence changed as the intensity of his eye contact made it feel like he was staring into my soul.

The long silence and eye contact was beginning to make me feel uncomfortable, so I began searching through the Rolodex of small talk topics in my head to keep the conversation moving. The train continued zipping along down the tracks, sunlight intermittently disrupted by the occasional passing building while I was scrambling, unable to think of anything. My mind still wasn't quite right and my ability to properly focus was clearly being affected.

"What is wrong with you?" he calmly asked.

I jerked my head back slightly, opening my mouth like I was going to quickly respond, but I had nothing to say. I was shocked by the nature of his question.

"Uhhhh……. ummmmm…...Uhhhhh" I made the sounds as I kept opening and closing my mouth, figuring eventually something would come out that made sense. It was something about the raspy, yet smooth tone of his voice mixed with the certainty he delivered the question with that really hit me. It was like he figured me out and had noticed with one quick passing moment of eye contact from across the train that I was having a bad day. Was this why he made a B-line towards me after entering the train?

I immediately had to fight back tears from forming in my eyes. With one confidently delivered line of questioning, he cracked my shell that I had spent years keeping intact.

I gathered myself internally and tried to play it off. Maybe I was reading too much into this and it was simply a language barrier problem getting the better of me. I thought that maybe he was actually trying to ask something different but didn't know how to properly word the question. I needed to approach this rationally.

"What do you mean?" I replied.

I was met by a long pause as I sat there, looking down and avoiding eye contact while running different options of what he might really be asking.

"You are in pain. Something is wrong with you" he said as he pointed to his head, indicating he knew I was going through something internally.

What the hell is happening here? My mind began racing with a million different thoughts and possibilities. Who is this guy? Am I on a prank show or something? This wasn't making sense and if it was supposed to be funny, it wasn't.

I was completely speechless while I ran through all the reasons this could be happening.

"So much pain in your eyes. Your face. You need help. You will be okay. Hold onto the beautiful things in life and make that your focus. Do not let sadness consume you. Smile. Be happy. You are young and have so much life to live. You will be okay."

This is when I lost the battle with the tears I had been holding back as one or two slipped out. I was in disbelief about what was occurring. Was this guy some sort of expert cold reader? What was his purpose for doing this? What was the end game here? I've been trying to deal with this in my own way privately and now here I am, crying in public while a stranger I've never met before tried to console me.

I looked back up at him, wiping the few tears from my eyes. "Why are you doing this? Why are you saying this to me?" His answer was simple.

"I see sadness because I know sadness, so I try to help sad people. People that are like how I used to be."

"Why were you sad? Are you not sad anymore?" I questioned him further as he looked at me with a slight smile on his face.

"The world is full of sadness and pain. I want to help change that. I was sad for far too long. Being sad and feeling pain is part of life but being stuck experiencing only those emotions is no way to live. My wife is gone now, so that made me sad. My friends are all gone too and that kept me sad. It was lonely. Now, I go to the hospital to treat cancer and maybe I will soon be gone too. I realize I must spend the rest of the time I have trying to be happy, enjoying all that life has given me rather than focusing on what it has taken. I must be strong and set an example of how to live the best life possible for those who remain after me. Like my children and their children. Like you."

He dropped these words of wisdom on me as if he had rehearsed them many times before. His delivery was smooth, and he had clearly taken the time to think this line of thought out very well. Meanwhile, I was stuck sitting there, unable to respond, completely confounded, and without words at all. He continued to look at me with that ever-present slightly crooked smile while we sat for a rather long time in complete silence, listening only to the train racing over the tracks, feeling the air pressure change as we went past buildings, tunnels, or other passing trains, zooming towards our final destination.

I didn't have a good way in this moment to process what was happening. Here I was, sitting with my headphones in trying to drown out a world I felt nothing for, and this old man spots me. Then, despite all of his own personal hardship, he goes above and beyond to try and make me feel better. I wondered how often he did this. Did he just have some innate drive to assist those he felt are in need of help? I mean, I've pulled over to help people change tires or assisted where I can during my life but doing what he was doing is on another level.

As I pondered more about the man sitting in front of me, I came to realize how comforting his presence was. He embodied the role of a father figure. He was calm and thoughtful even when dealing with my chaotic and frenzied thoughts. It was like he was guiding me to a resolution that had been right there all along, but I just needed some help getting there, and he was happy to show me the way.

I looked back up at the man, finally deciding I should stop staring at the ground and look him in the eye.

I knew I needed to say something back eventually. We couldn't sit in silence forever and I could only handle the intensity of his stare for so long. However, I also knew that I wanted to cry. He really dug something up that I had buried deep and having it all surface at once was a bit much, albeit necessary. I couldn't run from these problems forever. I had to confront them at some point, right? There is no time like the present, I guess.

"Thank you," I said with a shaky voice. A disappointing response I'm sure, but it was all I could muster. Despite my best efforts, I genuinely had no idea what to say in this given situation but saying nothing felt even worse than just awkwardly thanking him.

"You're welcome, my friend," he responded, bowing his head slightly, still smiling.

The train began to slow. The hum of the engine began to deepen as the brakes engaged and the brightness of the still early morning sun disappeared behind the overhangs of the outdoor platforms of the station we were pulling into.

For these last few minutes, I had forgotten where we were. In my mind, it had been just me and him. As all the other noises of the train began to dull, I was met with the sounds of conversation and the collective noise of people beginning to move towards the sliding doors, ready to exit. I took a moment to gather myself, trying to see what stop we were at and realized that we had gone through several stops during our conversation. Now there were quite a few more people on the train. In fact, it had been nearly 30 minutes and the final stop where I was getting off in Kyoto was only a few away.

"This stop is mine for the hospital," he said suddenly, pulling me from my shock. He slowly got up, using his cane to support him, hand shaking while he used all his effort to push himself up from the seat. He turned and started to walk away while I just sat there watching, like a deer in headlights, completely frozen. The train finally came to a complete stop and the doors opened to the concrete platform where more people were standing, waiting for passengers to first get off the train before they got on and occupied the newly emptied seats.

The old man took a few steps towards the doors as the crowd slowly exited. Just before he got too far away, he turned back to me and said, "Make today a good one. Smile. You will be okay."

"Thank you! Goodbye." I responded.

"Bye-bye," He now smiled from ear to ear as he waved at me and bowed before turning back to leave. I smiled and slightly bowed my head in return as he walked through the doors and disappeared on the platform into a crowd of people.

I was still unsure what to make of the experience I just had, but for the first time in days, I felt okay. I felt the weight of the world lifting off my shoulders. The words that he said, and his presence calmed me. I wasn't fighting tears anymore. I was actually smiling.

I was okay.

I had the sudden urge to run off the train to chase after him and keep talking. He wasn't moving very fast. Even though there were now quite a few people, I could probably find him and maybe I could help him get to his destination. I wanted to learn more about him. It felt like I had just said goodbye to someone I had known for a lifetime.

That's it! I'm going after him. I shot up from my seat and grabbed my backpack from the overhead rack.

Just as I turned to make my mad dash the doors began to beep as the conductor came over the intercom, speaking the same monotone way an airline pilot does, giving information about the next stop. The doors quickly shut. My sudden movement had caught the attention of all the people now on the train as they looked at me, the foreigner, wondering what I was doing. I missed my chance and the train quickly began to move again. I let out an audible sigh as the train moved along, coming out from under the station canopy, pretending like I had just accidentally missed my stop as I sat back down, hugging my backpack while it sat on my lap.

For as speechless as I was during the conversation, I was filled with questions now. Questions that I will never get to ask. I looked out the windows of the train, watching objects pass by faster and faster while we picked up speed. I looked back watching the station get smaller and just as it began to leave my field of view, I whispered to myself. "Goodbye, and thank you."

Reflection

At first, I thought that this was a crazy old man who probably just did this to people and mostly got ignored. Then, when he tried his gimmick on me, I was in just the right mindset to believe everything he said. It was like he was playing a numbers game and he won the lottery with me on that day.

Next, I honestly wondered if this was some sort of divine intervention. I am not religious, but this almost made me go back to church for the first time since I was a kid. Almost.

Lastly and most likely, this man was telling the truth and was just incredibly in tune with other people's emotions. He saw something was wrong with me and he wanted to help. He is a good soul and wanted to make someone smile rather than allow them to sink lower in sorrow. This is the option I prefer to believe. I honestly doubt he woke up that morning thinking he would have such a lasting effect on someone through his actions, but he did. It is something I will carry with me and remember for the rest of my life.

Very rarely does more than a week go by without me thinking of this, despite it occurring several years ago. It is genuinely unexplainable to me. Whenever someone asks me what I make of it, I have never quite figured out a good way to answer that question. The only thing I can say for certain about this experience and its effects on me is that it helped me realize how simple actions made by good people can truly make a difference. I have become far more conscious of the difference I can make in someone's life, even a stranger's. His actions were contagious and if I can continue to spread that to others, no matter how big or small a difference is made, I think the world would be a little better for it.

I have actually gone back to Japan several times since this event, and I have ridden this very same train several more times as well. I always try to sit in the same place, hoping that somehow this man will sit back down next to me again and we can finish our conversation. Maybe I can finally give him a proper thank you for pulling me out of the hole I had sunk into. I know the reality of what most likely happened to him since this event occurred. I know he is probably no longer with us, but I still have hope he is out there, somehow, continuing to lift people up the way he did for me.

I'm sad that I never got to learn even his name. He shall be forever known to me as the man on the train, but I shall forever be thankful to him for the difference he made for me.

Thank you and goodbye, my friend.......

THE GHOST IN THE BASEMENT

Nate

I always hated my basement. I admit that it isn't overly creepy, and nothing in particular stands out as abnormal. It's a standard, half-finished, run-of-the-mill basement. Except for one small detail. It's haunted. Like, super haunted.

A few of my friends and I were the original ghost hunters. Long before it became a popular TV trend to go around in haunted places to try and film encounters with the supernatural, we were doing it in my basement.

From the very first day we moved into that house when I was little, something bothered me about that basement. It just felt off. I would only go down there out of absolute necessity, such as doing laundry or retrieving something when asked to do so. Otherwise, it might as well have been marked off with yellow crime scene tape. I always had the feeling that I was being watched or I would see figures standing near me, catching them out of the corner of my eye, only to turn and they would no longer be there. I had an awareness of something's presence, despite there being no one around.

For the longest time, I kept my haunted basement a secret from my friends. Until one day, for no reason in particular, I spilled the beans to my best friend Mike. I regretted telling him immediately. Not only did he not believe me, but he made fun of me for even suggesting ghosts existed. Like any other 14-year-old kid does in these situations, I couldn't just let it go. Instead, I set out to prove it to him.

A few days after my big ghostly reveal, I told Mike to come over to the house when my parents weren't home. Once he arrived, I revealed to him my simple plan that would make a believer out of him.

"Alright, all you have to do is go down into the basement and hang out down there alone for a while. Take as much or as little time as you need, and you will see how haunted it really is." I explained to him.

"That's it? That's all I have to do?" he responded, looking at me with kind of a smug expression on his face.

"Yup, that's it. Unless you're too scared or something?" I quipped back quickly with my own smug face to match, confident this was all it would take.

I knew what it was like to be down there alone. I knew that this would be enough to make a believer out of him. I don't recall a single time ever going down into the basement and not having at least a little something creepy happen. I especially never wandered alone down there by myself. I feel like that's just asking for it, so it was only natural that that's what I was having him do. It was a bit of a gamble, but I was certain it would pay off.

Mike started heading downstairs, acting like it was no big deal. I'm not sure whether he was just putting on a brave face or if he genuinely didn't believe me, but either way my plan to get him down there alone worked. He got down to the bottom of the steps and turned back to me.

"You really think there are ghosts down here? Like, seriously?" he asked me.

"Not a doubt in my mind."

"Whatever." He turned back and walked through the door and out of sight.

I sat on the couch, awkwardly silent while Mike walked around my basement alone. I couldn't really hear anything going on, but I remember having very mixed emotions about the entire ordeal. I firmly believed my basement was haunted. I wanted something to scare the hell out of my friend to prove that I wasn't completely crazy. At the same time though, I didn't want anything too crazy to happen because it would just make my already crippling fear of the basement worse by confirming it was haunted.

I waited patiently for quite some time, twiddling my thumbs, legs shaking up and down with nervous tension as nothing seemed to be happening. I started to lose hope and even began preparing myself to be ridiculed endlessly by my friends that were bound to hear about this later.

As more and more time passed, my anxiety about the situation grew. What if something happened? Should I go check on him? Is that what he wants me to do so that he can jump scare me when I go down there? Ugh, this was getting frustrating.

I couldn't take it anymore. I was just about to get up from the couch when I heard Mike, somewhere down in the basement still, let out a high-pitched shriek, which was immediately followed by a loud thump against one of the walls. Next came a series of thuds and shattering glass as Mike began screaming every obscenity under the sun. I began hearing his footsteps getting louder and faster as he got back to the bottom of the steps. I began to move towards the stairs to see what was happening and make sure he was okay.

"What the fuck? What the fuck? What the fuck? What the fuck?" Mike quickly repeated in a shaky, exasperated tone of voice. He sounded truly scared. This wasn't a prank. Something happened. He flew up the steps, making large leaps, skipping the majority of them, and was to the top of the stairs before I knew it.

"What happened?" I questioned him. He didn't even look at me. Without the slightest hesitation, he shoved me out of the way, turned, and sprinted out my front door.

"What do I do?" I thought to myself. I was panicked. I then realized whatever happened down there wasn't done just yet. Standing at the top of the steps, staring down into the darkness of the basement beyond the doorway, I could hear something moving around, scratching against the walls. It was all the motivation I needed. I turned and flew out the front door to follow. By the time I got outside the door, I could see Mike in a full sprint, way ahead of me. He had already crossed the street and was cutting through the neighbor's yard, heading in the direction of his house, which was not too far away. I slammed the door behind me and abandoned ship, sprinting as fast as I could to catch up.

When I got to Mike's house, he was still outside. We were both completely exhausted, hands on our knees, trying to catch our breath. I was surprised to find him outside still. I honestly figured that based on how scared he was, he would have gone and locked himself in his room or something. Then I remembered his room was in the basement and I got the sense from him he wasn't in the mood for basements at the moment.

As I started to catch my breath I asked, "What happened? Why did you run like that? You okay?" But he just looked at me out of the corner of his eyes, shaking his head rapidly back and forth as he paced around his front yard. It was clear he didn't want to talk about it yet. I didn't really know what to do next. The only thing I did know, was that going back to my home alone wasn't an option, so we both just sat outside his house, enjoying the nice summer day while waiting for him to calm down.

It felt like forever, but after damn near an hour of sitting in silence, Mike finally looked like he was ready to talk. He opened his mouth as if he was going to speak before closing it again. I leaned in, ready to hear his story and finally figure out what happened to him down there. He shut his eyes and had to take a deep breath as if he was preparing to reveal a major secret. This was harder for him than I thought it would be. I patiently waited as he opened his eyes, centered himself, and began to tell me everything.

"I walked around for a few minutes and nothing was happening, so I started to get bored. I figured it would be freakier if it was dark, so I went around and shut all of the lights off. I went over to the finished section with all the spare furniture and grabbed a metal folding chair that was leaning against the wall. Then I sat down and just waited in the dark." Mike took a deep breath again at this point, preparing himself to tell me what happened next. "Nothing was happening!" He said almost sounding upset or frustrated. "I was just about quit and tell you that you were being a wuss. I got up from the chair and turned around to fold it up. Then out of nowhere a chill ran through my whole body starting from my head all the way down to my toes. It felt like I was paralyzed and couldn't move, dude. I heard a noise behind me, so I forced myself to turn around and look but there was nothing there. That's when I swear to God, I felt something standing right next to me, breathing down my neck as it whispered in my fucking ear! I was freaking out but tried to calm down and tell myself I was just hearing things, so I just paused and leaned against the chair to try and stand as still as possible. After a few seconds or so I heard something like a finger with long nails tap against the wall near me. I turned to see what it was, but then the folding chair was ripped out from under me and went flying backward, slamming into the wall. It scared me so bad I basically yelped and that's when I started trying to run. Before I could move though I felt that presence standing behind me again and I froze. I waited for a second again but then something screamed 'GOOOOOOOO' into my ear. I freaked out, man. I completely lost my shit and I thought I was going to die. I knew I needed to run, but it was like I lost all coordination and I just kept tripping every couple of steps. I tried to grab onto an end table to balance myself, but I knocked it over and I think I broke a lamp. Finally, I got my legs under me and I took off as fast as I could. I think the chair moved again too, but I'm not completely sure and then I went up the stairs to get the hell out of there. I don't ever want to go back."

I stood there listening to this with my jaw on the ground. All of the sounds I heard matched his story identically. Was the taping on the walls that he described what I heard after he bolted out the door? Maybe my basement didn't have a ghost, but instead, it was Satan himself. Whatever it was, it was no Casper the friendly ghost from what I could tell.

I looked over at Mike, not really sure how to properly respond to everything he just said. I decided to ask one very simple question.

"Can I stay here tonight?"

"Yeah" he replied.

After giving my brain a bit of time to begin processing everything Mike just said, questions started to swirl around in my head. My worst thoughts of what this could be were getting the best of me. I had to know more.

"What was the first thing it whispered in your ear? Was it a man or woman's voice? Are you positive it was a tapping on the walls and not, like, sounds from pipes or something from within the walls?" I probed.

"Woah, dude. Calm down." Mike quickly shot back at me, almost offended that I would dare question what happened to him. "The first voice was more of a whisper and I couldn't tell if it was a guy or girl. It was like it spoke to me in my own head, going from ear to ear rather than something actually standing next to me whispering. Like it whispered into my mind or something. It doesn't make sense, I know."

"No, no, no. I get it. For some reason that actually makes sense to me, but what about the second time? The one that screamed for you to go. What was that like?" I was desperate for answers.

"Ummmmm, that one was something straight up screaming into my ear. Like, I don't understand how you didn't hear it too."

A shiver shot down my spine. "It was that loud?" Mike just stood there looking at me, wondering why I kept questioning him. There was no doubt in his mind what had happened, and I think my questions were starting to either annoy him or make him relive the events too much.

"Yeah, it was that loud."

On that note, Mike and I finally decided to get up and go inside where I made a B-line for the phone to call my mom and ask her if I could sleep over at Mike's that night. Next on the agenda, we called our friends Nick and Chris, telling them to come over and hang out for a bit since we had some crazy stuff to tell them.

Not long after, both of them showed up on their bikes. We were going to wait to tell them until after we made some plans or something, but this was like the secret I couldn't wait to reveal. The second they got off their bikes and walked up the driveway a bit I blurted it out.

"MIKE GOT ATTACKED BY A GHOST AT MY HOUSE!"

As one would expect, they stopped in their tracks looking mildly confused.

"Wait, sorry. Let me back up. My house is haunted, and Mike didn't believe me, so I told him to go down there alone and then something attacked him!" My more detailed explanation didn't help explain anything really as they still just stood there looking back and forth from me to Mike looking for someone to say what was actually going on.

"What? Nick asked plainly.

"Yeah, what are you talking about? Are you being serious?" Chris followed up quickly.

"Ugh……" Mike let out an exhale filled with disappointment that I spilled the beans so soon and didn't give us a chance to set it up properly at all.

"Yeah. Let's go inside and I will tell you what happened."

Once inside, Mike sat down and told them everything. Every little detail about the ghost whispers, tapping on the walls, lamps breaking, and chairs being thrown. Both Nick and Chris sat there mesmerized, hanging onto every single word as Mike gave his best recollection.

"And that's it. That's everything." Mike said, wrapping up his story.

What happened next was a bit unexpected, to say the least. I thought Nick or Chris or both of them might just laugh at us or call us idiots, liars, or much worse. Instead, they wanted to try.

"Can we go over there and sit down there, too?" Nick asked.

"Wait, you want to have that happen to you????" Mike seemed astonished.

"Not tonight guys. My parents will be home from work soon but maybe tomorrow if you guys can stay too?" I was on board. The more people who believed me, the less crazy I was.

So, we set a plan. Nick and Chris called home to get permission to stay over at Mike's. The following day we would be going ghost hunting. It was summertime and we were still only in High School, so every night was basically the weekend and during the week, everybody's parents were gone at work. This meant my basement was free for investigation at least 5 days a week.

The four of us sat up all night watching Dragonball Z reruns and making our plan of attack to investigate the ghosts and prove they were real. It was decided that we would use Mike's video camera and set it up in my basement for different lengths of time. All of us agreed to go up to my room and be completely quiet while the filming took place. We genuinely wanted to figure out what happened to Mike in that basement. I also selfishly wanted to figure out if I needed to move out and never return or risk being killed by some sort of demon. It was a very delicate and precarious situation for me in particular.

Morning came to us with little sleep, but we were determined. We were kids, so operating on little sleep, especially during the summer, was basically what we did all the time. Around 8 A.M., once my parents had gone to work, we all walked over to my house and got all of our equipment set up, and by equipment, I mean the single camera that we had. Upon walking downstairs to figure out where to put the camera and film, we examined the basement together, immediately spotting the broken lamp, which luckily my parents must not have spotted the previous night. The first order of business was to get that cleaned up. It was a junky old lamp anyway, left behind by one of my sisters that moved out years before, so it wouldn't be missed.

The next priority was determining the filming setup and how we wanted to capture the ghosts on camera. We walked around looking for good spots to set everything up. I assume this is similar to what a hunter does in the woods when setting up trail cameras looking for wild game, except we were hunting spirits from another dimension.

My basement was half finished and half unfinished, separated by a long dividing wall connected by two doorways on either side. On the finished side was where Mike was attacked in the space where my sister formerly used as her room before going off to college. After that it led to a workshop used by my Step-Dad to work on, fix, or fit new golf clubs as a side business. The unfinished side was long and narrow. One end was used mostly for laundry, while the other side had wall-to-wall boxes and storage with only a narrow-ish walking path leading to the other side where there was a door to the workshop, along with another door that had stairs leading to the connected garage.

To help illustrate, here is a nice little drawing that can be referenced for the remainder of the story to see which area is being talked about.

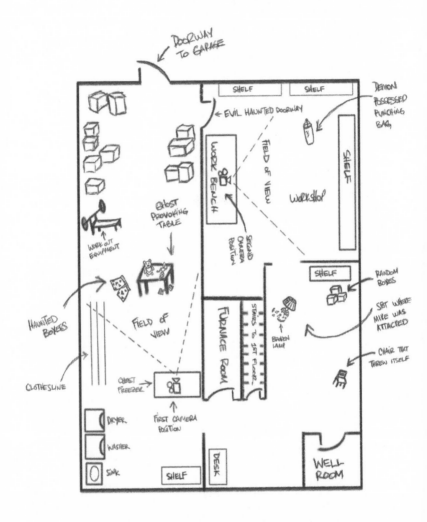

The choice became obvious for the first camera position. We had an extra chest freezer in the basement that laid flat and made for a perfect low-budget camera stand. There was only one thing left to do. We set the camera down, turned it on, hit record, and walked away. We closed the door to the basement and went up to my room where we would sit for five minutes.

The tension was palpable. Everyone was completely quiet, only occasionally looking up at one another, exchanging awkward glances. I'm not sure anyone really knew what to expect. It wasn't like we thought some sort of skeleton or apparition would appear or pop up and wave at the camera declaring it was real. However, some part of me secretly wanted exactly that to happen at the same time. Between what I had experienced and what had happened to Mike, I genuinely thought we were on to something and I didn't want that all to suddenly stop or come to an end. I was willing to do pretty much anything to prove these ghosts were real and that I wasn't crazy. So, there we sat, alone with our thoughts, wondering what kind of nonsense we would capture only a few feet below us.

"This is weird," Nick whispered.

"Shhhhhhhh." Mike quickly snapped back at him. I think he felt the same as me.

After the longest five minutes of my life went by, it was finally time to retrieve our evidence and see what we found. We cautiously went downstairs, looking around each corner to make sure the ghosts weren't still waiting to kill us in front of the camera we set up to capture them. We did a quick once-over around the filming area. Nothing seemed amiss. It made me feel very torn and conflicted. On one hand, any normal child would be relieved that nothing happened since few people are happy to learn they live with ghosts. On the other hand, if we didn't capture anything, Mike and I would look absolutely crazy, while Nick and Chris would be sure to ridicule us and probably tell other people. I pushed these thoughts out of my head as we grabbed the camera and rushed back upstairs to my room.

I turned the T.V. on and hooked the camera up using the old-fashioned red, white, and yellow audio/video cables. The blue screen of the camera display pulled up on the screen as we rewound the tape to the beginning. Mike operated the buttons and nodded to everyone that it was ready. We all nodded back as he looked down and pushed play.

The picture came up on the screen. The lighting of the basement was very Blair Witch style since we used the built-in night vision. Everything had a slight glow to it in kind of a greenish hue. The camera focused on the long unfinished side of the basement, looking at all of the stacks of boxes along with some workout equipment on the left side of the wall, while other junk was laid along the right side, leading all the way to the doors on the other side. The door leading to the garage was a white metal door and was always kept closed, while the door to its right, leading into the workshop, was always left open. At the top left-hand corner of the screen, you could also see part of a clothesline with several pieces of clothing currently drying on each line.

Our eyes stayed glued to the screen as the timer at the bottom right-hand corner ticked by, slowly counting upwards towards the 5-minute mark. I was sweating through my t-shirt. Any moment now, that skeleton was going to pop up and wave at the camera. It felt like reeling in a fishing lure knowing that at any second the biggest fish you have ever caught was going to bite. We were on the precipice of something big. But unfortunately, reality soon struck us over the head. Hard. There was no big fish on the line. No skeleton waving at the camera. Nothing. It was just four kids sitting there, staring at a screen, letting their imaginations get the better of them while playing back video from a budget camera with a budget night vision lens, watching absolutely nothing happen.

Time was up and the screen went black. We should have known better. Of course, a bunch of teenagers thought they were going to strike gold with the very first attempt. What kind of patience level can one realistically expect of a bunch of teenagers? Nick and Chris immediately seized this opportunity to make fun of us.

"I knew nothing was going to happen all along. You guys are being babies." Chris spoke so confidently now.

"Yeah. This idea was dumb. I was just playing along, but I was never actually scared." Nick said as smug as ever.

Mike and I knew otherwise. After they wouldn't relent with the name-calling, we called them out on their fake little act.

"If it is no big deal and you aren't scared, then maybe you guys can do what Mike did and go down there one-by-one by yourselves? It would help prove there is nothing down there," I said in a mocking tone, trying to goad them on.

"NO WAY!" They both spoke over one another immediately.

"That's what I thought."

With that settled, it was time to figure out what our next plan of action was. We weren't giving up just yet. After spending some time getting Nick and Chris back on board with the idea of ghost hunting, we conducted a solid brainstorming session to determine our best course of action.

Eventually, Mike came up with an idea that everyone immediately agreed with. We needed to provoke and piss the ghost off! Also, we needed to put stuff out in front of the camera's field of view that can easily be moved or manipulated, like a ghost-provoking table, or something that had items sitting on it that could be moved or manipulated easily. We spent a decent amount of time hashing out the many details of our plan, but in the end, it could basically be simplified like this:

Step 1: Put stuff in front of camera. Step 2: Piss off ghost/demon. Step 3: watch the ghost/demon throw or move the stuff we placed out. Brilliant, right? It was flawless teenager ghost hunting logic.

We went back down in the basement and grabbed an old card table that had been sitting around for years. We placed it about 10 feet in front of the camera's recording position and then set out lightweight, non-breakable items on the table that could easily be pushed off or moved without too much effort. For example, a stuffed animal or an action figure. I also grabbed one of my dumbbells that could easily roll and placed it under the table, resting it against one of the legs, ensuring that it could only roll in one direction. I'm not sure why we thought this was the best way to set it up, but we did. We also made sure to film ourselves setting everything up. That way, after we got famous for capturing the first-ever real ghost encounter on camera, if someone suggested that we rigged something to happen, they could watch for themselves that we did no such thing.

Before leaving the room to film our new flawless setup, it was time to piss off some ghosts. Mike refused for obvious reasons regarding his earlier encounter. Nick and Chris both thought it was a dumb idea, but at least they were admitting it up front this time. They were also very aware they were being filmed, which would likely result in the worst kind of ridicule; the kind that could be watched over and over again while everyone laughs at how dumb you looked. This meant it was my turn to put on a brave face. I honestly didn't have much of a choice if this was going to work, so I took a deep breath, walked out from behind the camera, and started speaking to anything willing to listen.

"Okay, you bitch ass ghost! If you really want to show us you're real, then do something! Move an object on this table. Move these weights. Just don't suck and not do anything at all because I'm starting to think you don't exist anymore. Hell! Even Mike is starting to think you don't exist anymore. So, prove it. You have 10 minutes to do whatever you want. Don't hold back!"

I went all in and didn't hold back no matter how dumb it made me look. At least I could look back at this if nothing happens and say I gave it my all. I thought I did a pretty good job. As I walked back behind the camera and we started to head upstairs again, all of the guys were kind of chuckling under their breath having just watched me talk to potentially imaginary ghosts, but I didn't care. I did what needed to be done.

We set our timer when we got to my room and once again, watched the seconds tick by while we waited for the 10 minutes to pass. I was certain that if nothing happened this time, we would probably be forced to give up. This was as good as it was going to get. I remember while we sat there silently, hearing nothing but the slight ringing in my ears, I was focusing on trying to hear any type of noise come from the basement. Sound carried pretty easily through the house, especially from the basement through the heat vents in the floors, but I heard nothing. I was actually beginning to regret the entire thing, worried that I was going to simply become known as the weird ghost boy or something among my friends, but at least Mike would be part of the group too, I guess.

The 10 minutes went by quickly enough. We walked downstairs, this time not as cautiously, feeling a bit more confident that nothing was going to happen anyway, but when we turned the corner, our jaws all dropped. We finally saw what we were looking for, although not exactly what we had expected. I was the first to notice that the dumbbell had rolled across the floor to the other leg of the table before coming to a stop there. Nick pointed out that a pair of my boxers, which had been hanging from the clothesline, was now laying on the ground. All of us stopped moving forward. This was beginning to feel very real all of the sudden. We looked to one another, seeking reassurance that everyone was seeing the same thing.

"Was that closed when we started?" asked Chris. We all turned quickly to see what he was talking about. The doorway to the workshop at the other end of the basement had been closed. My family never closes that door. I honestly didn't even know if it could close. We each turned to one another waiting for someone to confirm that they had closed it, but no one spoke up.

"Duuuuude." Nick summed up what everyone was thinking in a single, simple word.

We didn't dare get any closer to the activity. Mike quickly took a few steps forward, snatched the camera off the freezer, and turned back to us walking like a speed runner doing their laps at the local mall. We followed him, going back upstairs and far away from the demon we now figured had been captured on camera. Once at the top of the stairs, Mike turned to go to my room, but Chris spoke up saying,

"Are we sure we really want to watch that here? You know, in the place where it happened?"

No one even bothered to respond, because it was the best idea anyone had suggested yet, so, Mike went to my room, basically ripped the audio/video cords from my T.V. and we all bolted out the door, experiencing a collective panic attack on the way back to Mike's house.

We plugged everything into the T.V. in Mike's living room, preparing ourselves to watch the haunting unfold on the screen. Before hitting play, Mike looked around one more time just like before, to make sure that everyone was okay with watching this. This time was different than last though. This time, we saw the aftermath of something. We knew we were going to witness something happen somehow. This time the fish was on the line and all we needed to do was reel it in. Maybe the skeleton did raise from the ground and wave at the camera. We just had no idea. We all nodded, anxiously awaiting what was going to happen. He took yet another deep breath.

"Here we go." He hit play.

The screen lit up once again, showing the same view we had become familiar with from before, with that same green hue. The only difference was our nice provoking table set up, clearly within view of the camera. Minutes went by with absolutely nothing happening.

"Come on. Something happen," Nick said impatiently. We all knew as we sat there with bated breath that at any moment, something had to happen. It was no longer if, it was when. We were desperately wanting to know what caused everything to happen. Why was the door closed? How did the dumbbell move? Why were my boxers on the ground?

Five minutes went by and then six with nothing happening. The thought crossed my mind that we should fast forward until we see something happen, but I knew we might miss something. It wasn't worth the risk. The moment where I was the most impatient, waiting for potentially life-changing events to occur, was when I needed patience the most. But time was running out as we watched the nine-minute mark pass and that's when it finally happened. A light clicked on from the workshop on the other side of the dividing wall where the camera wasn't able to see. We could only see the light, shining through the doorway at the end of the room.

Now, let me take a moment to explain something about this particular light because it is important to understand. The switch itself is positioned to flip right or left rather than up or down like most light switches, making it more like a breaker switch on a fuse panel than it does a standard light switch. What I'm trying to say is, much like a breaker switch, it is difficult to flip into the on and off position and requires a bit of force. Also, if you've ever flipped a breaker switch before, you would know how loud they can be and that applies to this switch as well.

There was no mistaking it. As the light flipped on and began shining through the doorway, we could hear the switch audibly flip positions in the video. The noise caused us all to jump back from the screen. It took a moment to register that we just watched a light turn itself on, but before we could even comment on it, the switch could audibly be heard flipping again, this time turning the light back off. Our eyes widened and most of us sat there, mouths open, shocked at what we saw. We all stared at one another in disbelief because obviously none of us could have known this would happen. We knew we would have evidence yet to come, but no one expected this.

"Guys!" Nick said drawing our attention back to the screen.

We all watched, eyes drawn to the doorway where the light had just recently been emanating from the switch that turned on and off as the door to the workshop slowly closed shut. Normally in scary movies, you always hear a door slam from some unknown location within the house, usually intended to get a jump scare out of you. This was not like that at all. It wasn't quick or abrupt. Imagine instead, you were trying to sneak out of the house quietly without anyone noticing, so you close the door as slowly as possible to not make any noise. You may even turn the handle to ensure no click happens when the latching mechanism slides into place. That is how the door closed itself on its own. It was absolutely horrifying to watch, sending chills down my spine. I could immediately picture this happening while I was asleep at night. Hell, maybe it had already done this before and then it just stood at the end of my bed, deciding whether or not that was the night it would choose to kill me.

While I sat there picturing the demon at the end of my bed, another 10 seconds go by and the pair of boxers, held up by clothespins were suddenly yanked from the clothesline and fell to the ground. The line was left bouncing up and down from the force exerted to pull the boxers down. Next, our attention was quickly drawn to the table we had set up with objects and we watched as the dumbbell positioned against the leg of the table, slowly started to roll, bit-by-bit, inch-by-inch, before coming to a rest against the opposite leg of the table.

There were only 30 seconds left before our unsuspecting former selves would begin making our way into the basement. Everything had been happening so fast all of a sudden that to have even 5 seconds of silence felt like an eternity. There was too much time to think. It was like knowing the end of the movie and wanting to scream at the characters in the film to stop and just stay away since you knew the fate that awaited them. Little did we know, that the worst was still yet to come. We thought we knew the ending to the movie, but we had no idea.

THUMP. THUMP. THUMP.

The room fell silent. No one even dared to breathe.

THUMP. THUMP. THUMP.

A few more seconds passed and now the noise of our former selves could be heard making their way into the hornet's nest that was my haunted basement.

"What the fuck was that?" Nick asked.

"I don't know. Hold on a second" Mike replied while fiddling with the camera controls, desperately trying to rewind so we could watch again. He finally managed to go back a few seconds and we turned the volume up almost as high as it would go. All you could hear was loud white noise.

THUMP. THUMP. THUMP. There it was again! A few more seconds passed.

THUMP. THUMP. THUMP.

Then, something else came into the mix that we didn't hear the first time around. Something was whispering. Just off camera where we couldn't see, there was an unintelligible otherworldly noise that sounded like several people whispering over one another. It was like walking into a lunchroom where everyone was sitting having their own conversations among their group. You can't make out any one particular voice, but only hear the collective white noise it creates. If you take that noise and turn it into a whisper, you would hear what we were hearing.

Mike hit the stop button and the screen went black. He turned to us, looking pale and mortified. "I know what the thud noise was on the camera," he said as he stared, off looking at no one in particular. We thought he might have a rational explanation for what we just heard.

"Something was playing with the microphone, tapping it as you do for a mic check. I've done it before when filming other stuff and it's exactly the same. I swear."

The room stayed silent. We didn't know what to do next. Clearly, I was never going back home ever again. In fact, I remember trying to devise ways in my head to convince my parents to let me move in with Mike. It didn't matter to me how far-fetched of an idea that was. I never wanted to go back to my house ever again. I regretted ever telling Mike about the stupid haunting. I wanted everything to go back to the way it was before I said anything, so I could just keep my mouth shut while living blissfully ignorant that my house was haunted by ghosts who could close doors, turn lights on, move weights, and tap camera microphones.

It took a while for everyone to calm down from the excitement and terror of what we just watched. It probably didn't help that we watched the video several more times, doing our best to make sense of the nonsensical. We debated about what to do next, but Mike came through again, cutting through the noise and arguing with another solid suggestion.

"We have to go back and see if we can find a logical explanation for some of the stuff that happened."

In other words, just like all the ghosts shows on today, we were going to take the time to go back to the scene and debunk everything we could. Hopefully, we could prove everything wrong so I could actually sleep at night. I no longer cared if everyone thought I was crazy. I just wanted life to go back to normal.

We finally mustered up the courage and headed back to my house. Once inside, we headed for the staircase, getting to the top of the steps before all of us noticed something was wrong. We could hear a loud noise coming from the basement. It was the sound of chains, creaking and clinking together along with some sort of low growling, grinding noise. We all turned to each other confirming that everyone was hearing the same thing. However, despite hearing the same thing, my reaction was different. Everyone else expressed curiosity as I shook my head back and forth, stepping backward out of fear while everyone looked at me, concerned by my actions. Much like Mike's familiarity with his camera and the noises it makes, I was familiar with sounds that occurred in my basement. I knew exactly what the noise was, but it didn't make sense. I decided to put on my brave face and quickly started down the stairs before I could change my mind as everyone followed close behind. Once at the bottom, instead of turning right towards the freezer and where everything had been set up, I did a U-turn to the left. The other side of the basement, the finished side, is like a wide hallway. There is a ton of leftover crap from when my sisters moved out sitting over to the right. This is where Mike was attacked previously. At the end of the hallway is the other doorway entrance into the workshop.

I stopped in my tracks as I looked down the hallway into the workshop and couldn't believe what I was witnessing. I yelled at Mike to turn the camera on and record. At first, he looked confused but quickly caught on as he fumbled with the buttons in his panicked state. After finally managing to hit record, he finished making his way down the stair to meet us.

I remember watching the film later. It begins looking down at Mike's feet as he gets to the bottom of the stairs before panning up to see the three of us. It only focuses on us for a second before turning the corner, panning to the left, and looking down the hallway into the workshop. The light was back on and there in the back corner of the workshop was my punching bag, swinging end to end, ceiling to ceiling, from the chain it was hung from. The next few seconds were silent. We just watched the grainy film as the bright white fluorescent lights of the workshop lit up my 80-pound black Everlast punching bag, chains grinding together as it violently swung back and forth.

Now, Nick was the one who started moving first as we followed towards the workshop. How we managed not to just turn and run right then and there, still boggles my mind to this day. If this was a horror movie, this was the part where you scream at the T.V., telling everyone they should just get out while they can. The camera stays focused on Nick as he leads the way. He moved forward almost like he was trying to sneak up on the punching bag as he cautiously entered the workshop, quickly looking left and right to make sure nothing was waiting there for him. The punching bag continued swinging side to side as if someone had used every bit of force in their body to accomplish what we were witnessing. I'm not actually confident we could recreate this if we tried, since none of us were probably strong enough. It was starting to lose a bit of momentum by the time we all finally entered the room, but it was still shocking to see. It just didn't make sense. Nick, still being the brave one of us walked up to the bag and gave it a giant bear hug as it slammed into him, knocking him back a bit. He walked it slowly forward and stopped all of its momentum. It was no longer moving, but we all sat there and stared at it, no one making a sound, like we were waiting for it to begin swinging on its own again.

The camera kept rolling and we all knew exactly what had to be done next. Mike set the camera down on the workbench, facing the punching bag, turned on the night vision, shut the light back off and we went upstairs to sit in silence for another 10 minutes.

We waited patiently for the minutes to pass, although it felt like time was standing still. I thought I was freaking out before. Ha! How little I knew of the world and its horrifying mysteries. My anxiety was through the roof. How was I going to convince my parents to move? That was the real question. Even more important, since they weren't going to buy the whole, "there is a ghost in the basement thing," I needed to come up with something compelling enough to do the trick, but what could that be?

"Time's up," Mike said calmly.

We went back downstairs, more cautiously than ever before, taking care with each step to make sure we didn't hear any other noises or somehow do something to make the ghost attack us next. No one was interested in becoming the human equivalent of the punching bag. However, this time, there was no swinging, no boxers on the floor, no dumbbells out of place, and all the lights remained off until they were turned on by us. There was nothing special of note. You could feel it too. Whatever magic we had captured before was gone. The air itself was no longer heavy and dark feeling like it always had been. It was probably one of, if not the only time I have ever walked into that basement and not felt scared for my life. It's hard to explain, but basically, our spider senses were no longer tingling.

Reviewing the tape only confirmed our suspicions. We saw nothing and we heard nothing. We were all back to having such conflicted feelings about the entire ordeal. We knew something happened. We all experienced it. We all felt it and it frightened us to the core when everything did happen. So, while we all wanted something to occur, at the same time, we felt a sense of relief that nothing was happening.

Unlike the literal door that we watched shut on camera earlier, our newly found sense of relief actually opened a figurative door for us to accomplish our original plan. Debunk everything that happened.

It seemed most logical to start with the most recent and shocking event, which was the punching bag. We all took turns walking up to it, pulling it back, and throwing it forward as hard as possible. None of us except Nick got even close to matching what we saw earlier. Also, it would lose momentum very quickly. Even on our best throws, by the next time it swung back it wouldn't come close to the original height. In addition to this, we kept having problems with the chain going slack at the top of each swing. Once it would reach its apex, the tension on the chain connecting the bag to the ceiling would relax just a bit and the bag would swing back down unevenly, resulting in a more erratic swinging motion. When we watched the bag swinging on its own earlier, it was like there was a constant two-way force being applied to the bag so that the chain never went slack. We kept attempting to throw the bag over and over again with no luck until I recommended we stop before something broke.

Ghost, 1. Humans, 0.

After getting the punching bag to finally stay still, we walked over to the light switch and each took turns messing with it, trying to find some sort of flaw with it that could cause it to flip on or off on its own. After screwing around with it for a while we realized that just like a fuse switch, although it gave a decent amount of resistance along its travel path, there was an area when the switch was basically neutral, that it could just sit in. We positioned the switch to this point and created a hypothesis. The last time someone was in that room they must have flipped the switch as they left the room.

However, they managed without knowing to place it perfectly in this middle ground or neutral area. Then slowly over time, the switch still pulled back to the on position, which just so happened to occur during our filming! It was genius.

"But, what about when it flipped itself back off?" Nick asked. In all of our excitement thinking we had debunked this, we had forgotten about that part. For this, we never came up with any rational solution. Hypothesis ruined.

Ghost, 2. Humans, 0.

We decided to move on and investigate the boxers. We hung them back up on the clothesline and each took turns pulling on them to see the amount of force required to actually pull them down while creating the same effect as we saw on the camera. We were actually able to recreate the effect fairly easily, but it didn't mean we had debunked it. Quite the opposite actually. If slow increasing force was applied, they would eventually pull off, but the clothesline would not bounce up and down afterward like it did in the video. This was only accomplished by pulling quickly. We came to the determination that the force used was sudden and quick. Once again, we couldn't find a rational explanation for this occurrence.

Ghost, 3. Humans, 0.

Next up was the dumbbell. We moved it back to the original position, resting against the leg on the right side of the table while we brainstormed for a bit, trying to think of what could have caused it to roll on its own. After standing there for a long time, occasionally making ludicrous suggestions, Chris was the first person to throw out a viable reason. "Maybe the floor isn't level!" he proclaimed. I sprang to action, running over to the workshop and grabbing a carpenter's level. We moved the table out of the way to make sure we were testing against the same spot where the weight rolled along. We waited patiently as the little bubble settled into place, determining if everything was as it seemed. As it turns out, Chris was on to something. The floor was not level. Unfortunately, the weights technically moved against the downgrade of the floor. In other words, they rolled ever so slightly uphill. Damnit.

Ghost, 4. Humans, still 0.

So, now between the punching bag swinging violently on its own, the light switch that turned on and off by itself, boxers that were yanked from the line, and weights that roll uphill, everyone was starting to feel more than just a bit uneasy.

"Hey, at least it's 4 vs. 1 in case it attacks," said Nick.

"Yeah, and we would still lose. It would drag us down to hell and make us all its bitch for all of eternity. Even if it was 400 of us, we still lose." Mike chimed in, putting a real damper on Nick's attempt at lightening the mood a bit.

Then, suddenly Mike walked away with a bit of a crazy look in his eye. He grabbed his camera and placed it on the freezer again, taking care to make sure it was set up just like before while we stood there wondering what he was doing. He turned it on and told everyone to be quiet. After hitting the record button and standing behind the camera in silence for a few moments, he took his index finger and began lightly tapping on the camera's microphone. The rest of us turned to each other nodding our heads as we finally realized he was trying to recreate the noises we heard in the video. Next, he took a few steps back and began his best attempt at making weird whispery sounds. He even waved his hands and arms around in a ghostly manner, doing his best to imitate whatever image he must have put in his head of what the ghost was doing behind the camera would have looked like. It was as ridiculous as it sounds.

Once he was done, we nervously started up the stairs to go hook up to the T.V. again and check out if Mike was right about what he said earlier. At this point, everyone was feeling pretty anxious to get out of the basement anyway after unsuccessfully trying to prove even a single thing rationally, so by this time, we were left with only our irrational thoughts.

As we sat in my room and Mike hit play, there was a palpable tension present again. Regardless of everything else that happened, for some reason, this was the one thing I remember wanting to be explainable. I wanted Mike's tapping sounds to be clearly different from what we heard earlier. The thought of some ghost from the past standing behind our camera, unable to fully understand the technology in front of it, therefore tapping a microphone out of confusion was something my teenage brain wasn't ready to deal with yet. If it could sneak up behind the camera at any moment like that, I felt like next time it would be me it snuck up behind and tap instead.

The screen came up and started off looking at Nick, Chris, and me with our eyes fixed on Mike, who by this point was already behind the camera, holding his finger to his lips telling us to be quiet. Here came the moment of truth. We turned the volume all the way up again.

THUMP. THUMP. THUMP.

No. No. No. No. No. No. No.

Nope. Nope. Can't deal. Nope. Nope. Nope.

My mind couldn't process it properly. The noises of his finger tapping on the mic were identical to the noises we had heard on the original film. Again, we all looked at each other knowing what this meant.

Ghost, 5. Humans, 0.

It became difficult to focus on the screen anymore for me. I was getting so paranoid, looking over my shoulder, waiting for some kind of nightmare come to life to be standing next to me.

Next came the whispering. However, Mike's attempt at making ethereal ghostly undead noises was unsuccessful. It was clearly a human voice just making odd sounds off-screen, looking ridiculous doing it and was clearly distinguishable. Unfortunately, I wouldn't necessarily call this a win for the humans though. It would be better classified as inconclusive because we didn't have a clear way of recreating anything. If it was anything at all, it was proof that humans can't make those noises so.......

Ghost, 6. Humans, still 0. It was a blowout.

So, where do we go from here? We had thoroughly proven the existence of these things in our mind by this time, so what could be left to do? I still hadn't thought of a viable excuse to move yet and we realized we were running out of time in the day. My parents would be home soon, so we had to make a choice on how to proceed. What was our next course of action?

Unfortunately, everyone was feeling a bit defeated and thoroughly freaked out at this point. Both Nick and Chris wanted nothing to do with this anymore. They had all the excitement they could handle. In fact, neither of them ever showed interest in doing this again. It is debatable as to why. Maybe they were too scared. Maybe they were genuinely no longer interested.

Mike and I waited until my parents got home so I could ask to stay at his place again. Thankfully they said yes. I wasn't ready to sleep in my own room yet. I kept picturing the door slowly opening and shutting without a sound as some horrifying disfigured demon stood over my bed watching me.

After spending another night, staying up far too late, recounting the events of that day, we waited for my parents to leave so we could try to capture the magic, or maybe it is better referred to as witchcraft, on camera again. For Mike and I, this became our obsession for quite a while. We would continue trying day after day after day. We filmed every single room from every single angle you can think of. We provoked, we prodded, and we waited, but we never saw anything ever again. Despite this leading to me finally sleeping peacefully again in my own house, it also resulted in frustration and feeling like we were wasting our summer. So eventually, we gave up our newfound hobby and went on with our lives.

When school eventually started up again and people asked what we had been up to all summer, we answered honestly and told them our ghost stories. As one might imagine, most people thought we were weird or crazy, so we ended up showing a lot of people the footage when they disputed our claims. Unfortunately, the majority of people who saw the tapes just thought we faked everything. A couple of people thought we were telling the truth and even asked to experience it themselves. I never followed through on their requests.

From this point on, I basically never went in my basement again unless absolutely necessary, back to status quo, I guess. Each time I did have to, it was always mixed feelings. Sometimes it felt fine, like I had made some sort of peace with the existence of some being down there, and other times I still feel like something malicious is down there, waiting for me. Just waiting for the moment it can finally strike. But, whether peaceful or malicious, I know that something is down there. I just no longer have the desire to find out for sure.

Reflection

As a kid going through High School, word got out pretty quickly about this whole thing and I actually became known for it. It was as close as I ever got to being popular. As an adult, I occasionally run into old classmates that clearly don't remember me. Adding salt to the wound, sometimes I run into the girls I used to have a huge crush on, and their lack of memory reminds me just how unmemorable I really was. Good to have perspective, I guess. As I sit there and try to help them remember me by giving them little details about who I was, it will suddenly click. You can see the light go off in their head. They will interrupt whatever I'm saying with, "Wait! You're the guy with the haunted basement, right?" I typically smirk, having purposely avoided bringing that up until this point. I guess it is better to be remembered for something weird like that than not be remembered at all. I just say yes and try to move on from it.

As I look back on it now, I still truly believe my parent's basement is haunted. I am a huge skeptic by nature, but my own personal experience living in that house gives more than just a little pause to that skepticism.

My parents still live in the house from the story to this day and I, as a grown man, still avoid going down there by myself unless I must. I can honestly say that we never faked any of it. Every single thing featured on those tapes is real and despite having 17 years pass since all of this occurred, I still can't explain any of it.

This series of events shaped how I have gone forward in my life in a major way. Once you experience something like this, it changes your perspective considerably. I'm far more paranoid than most of my friends. They hear a standard creaking of the walls when the wind blows a little too hard outside, but my mind interprets that as something crawling in the walls. I don't actually believe that, but any little noise, creak, crack, or otherwise gives me far more pause than the average person. I also hate watching scary movies because they just feel too real to me. I already have enough imagery in my head of ways a demon looks or methods by which it can kill me and watching scary movies only succeeds in making those nightmares feel a little more real.

I wish today that when I tell this story, that I still had those tapes. Maybe I could submit them to a T.V. show and have a film crew pick up where we left off to figure out what the hell is going on down there. Unfortunately, the tapes were destroyed about a year after we filmed everything. Despite being relatively well behaved as a kid, I did have a year or two where I went on a bit of a hellish streak. It certainly didn't help that during this time of my life, MTV's Jackass was a huge thing. We were young and easily influenced, plus we had a video camera, so it only made sense to our dumb teenage brains to film ourselves doing dumb stunts or pranks. However, while doing one of these stunts at about 3am on a weeknight with the same exact group of guys, we got caught. Each one of us was arrested and it was one of the most unpleasant experiences of my life. Worse yet, one of us that shall go unnamed (Chris…cough, cough) became very intimidated as he was questioned by the police. Therefore, rather than just confess that we did dumb stuff that night only, he felt the need to confess every wrongdoing we had ever done and then made sure to mention that we filmed all of it. Can you tell that 17 years later I'm still a bit salty about it?

Chris's unnecessary confession resulted in Mike going home after being released and immediately destroying every single tape he owned. He didn't have the time to differentiate between the tapes that were filled with stupid pranks and the ghost tapes. He burned them all. Looking back, we never did anything illegal on those tapes. In fact, the only reason we were arrested wasn't for our actions, it was just for the curfew violation of being minors out at 3am on a weeknight. Those tapes contained nothing more than a bunch of 15-year-old kids being complete idiots. Maybe the cops would have enjoyed watching the time we filmed Nick unknowingly drinking a soda filled with an insane amount of chili powder. Perhaps they would have laughed when Mike agreed to get hit in the nuts super hard. With hindsight always being 20/20, I wish Mike wouldn't have destroyed the tapes and while it wasn't necessary, I also understand why he did it. If it were me, I probably would have done the same. Just to add insult to injury, the cops never showed back up for the tapes anyway, so we destroyed them for nothing.

Maybe one day I will go back down there on another ghost-hunting mission and try my luck again. You never know. It might be fun.

UFO HIGH-SPEED PURSUIT

<u>Frank</u>

It was an uneventful Friday night where I lived. It was me and my friends Steve, Dave, and Chuck just driving around trying to make some last-minute plans. We were bored and desperately wanted something to do so we could enjoy the rest of the evening. It was a gorgeous fall night without a cloud in the sky as I looked out my driver's window, seeing nothing but stars above me. We didn't want to waste such a nice night by sitting inside and doing nothing, but we also had no idea what to do. All of us had already eaten and no one had enough spare cash to afford dessert. Our High School, which wasn't too far from my house was hosting the Homecoming football game, but that really wasn't our cup of tea either.

As we drove around aimlessly, I realized I was running low on gas. Unfortunately, not only was I short on cash for dessert, but I didn't have it for gas either, and ending such a nice night this early would have been a real bummer. Then I remembered that my cousin Jimmy, who didn't live far away, still owed me $3. He had been ducking me for weeks at this point and it was about time I showed up unannounced to collect his payment. How he had ever managed to get away for this long while owing me that much money was a miracle. It's important to remember that this was the early 70's and that $3 was going to go a long way when filing up the tank on my 1970 Dodge Dart Swinger.

It wasn't long until we arrived at my cousin's house. I told everyone to stay in the car since I was going to be quick. I knocked and my aunt quickly answered the door to let me in. "Hi, Aunt Mary! How have you been? Is Jimmy home?" I asked.

"Oh Frank, it is so good to see you! Yeah, he is home. Just go back to his room."

When I walked into my cousin's room, he knew why I was there, and he must have heard me talking to his mom because he already had the money ready in his hand. He knew I wasn't the type to show up unannounced, so my sudden arrival must have made my intentions clear. He also knew that although I was a polite guy, I really wanted that money, and he knew he'd been avoiding me, so it was time to pay up before my patience wore too thin.

After spending a few moments saying goodbye to my aunt, she shut the door behind me and I began walking towards my car, looking down lost in thought, determining which gas station was closest for me to fill up at. As I got closer, I looked up and noticed that everyone had gotten out of the vehicle and was nowhere to be found.

"Frank!" I heard my name being called. It sounded like it came from the side of the house, but I couldn't see anything. Everything around me was illuminated only by the moon and the stars since there were no streetlights in the area. I turned around, searching for where the voice came from as I began walking back towards the house. Finally, Steve popped out from around the corner and yelled, "Holy Shit, Frank! You've gotta come see this! Get over here!"

Steve wasn't normally a very excitable guy, but something clearly had him excited as I watched him bop around a bit before disappearing back around the corner of the house. I was so confused. I started walking in his direction, trying to think of what could be on the side of the house.

"Would you hurry up? Get over here! You're going to miss it!"

I can't recall any point in my life up to this point where I had seen Steve get like this. I took his advice and started jogging towards the side of the house and as I passed around the corner, I could see both Dave and Chuck frantically jumping up and down in excitement, cussing up a storm.

"Okay. I'm here. What's the big deal? Why did you guys get out of the car? What's happening? What's going on?" I asked desperately, never really giving anyone time to answer in between my barrage of questions. The excitement they were displaying was contagious. I really wanted to know what they were up to, but no one was answering me until I turned back to Steve. He was standing there, barely visible under what little light there was, looking up to the sky. He extended his arm and pointed his finger up.

"Look, dude."

The night sky above us was no longer visible. Instead, our view was obstructed by a massive saucer-shaped object, hovering directly overhead. It was no wonder that I didn't see it previously because it made absolutely no sound. There was no hum of an engine, no roar of a turbine, no whoosh of turning blades. Nothing. Complete and total silence that was only interrupted by our occasional gasps of shock and awe.

How is this possible? What the hell is this thing? What am I looking at? This wasn't making any sense and my brain couldn't keep up with processing the onslaught of thoughts running through my head as all four of us just stood there staring up at whatever this thing was.

I did my best to calm down and examine the object a bit more thoroughly. It was a circular shape with a diameter about as wide as 4 houses. It wasn't moving. It held its position perfectly. There were several different colored blinking lights located on different parts of it. As my mind tried its best to compute and crunch the numbers, the conclusion was becoming more and more clear. I was not looking at something from this world.

Steve broke the silence next. "It's a UFO! Holy shit! I can't believe it!" he said over and over again.

I turned to each one of my friends. They all stood there, jaws open wide, the whites of the widened eyes clearly visible. We were mostly speechless as Steve continued blabbering on in the background what everyone else was all thinking but maybe too afraid to admit to ourselves. The thought occurred to me that maybe we needed an adult to see this too and prove that we weren't all going crazy. I considered going back inside and grabbing my aunt to show her, but suddenly, the object started to move.

"Woah," said Chuck.

"How is it doing that?" Dave asked everyone.

"Doing what?" Steve quickly replied.

"You know......moving without making a sound? How is that possible?" Dave had caught on to what I was noticing as well.

We stood by and watched as the UFO crept along the sky slowly, eerily quiet. Even the effects of movement that one would expect were absent. It wasn't that high above us, yet there was no wind generated from it lifting up or moving away and no mechanical noises from it pitching upwards or changing directions. Thankfully, with it being such a clear night, even as it rose a bit higher, it didn't disappear behind any clouds and we were able to keep our eyes on it. Everyone knew what to do next. This was no longer going to be just another boring Friday night after all.

Everyone sprinted towards my car, which had been left running and was still a bit low on gas, but there was no time to think about that. I hopped into the driver's seat and threw it quickly into reverse not even taking the time to look for traffic as my foot pushed the pedal to the floor.

"Jesus, Frank!" Chuck shouted at me. I didn't realize that Steve hadn't even made it to the car yet and for those that did, they didn't have time to even close their doors, nearly being thrown from the vehicle as I whipped it around out of the driveway.

"LET'S GO!" I shouted at Steve as he finally made it to the car, and everyone finally managed to shut their doors. I gripped the wheel, knuckles turning white as I gunned it out of the neighborhood, tires screeching, engine roaring as we fish-tailed it out onto Main Street where we caught sight of the UFO again.

It hadn't gone far and had parked itself above the local strip mall, which wasn't far away. I blew the red light going into the parking lot of the mall. I wasn't letting this thing get away. This was the opportunity of a lifetime. As I slammed the brakes, sliding us into a parking space in the relatively empty lot, I remember thinking to myself that it was odd how obvious it was making itself. Why would it sit above such a well-lit spot? Were we the only ones who had noticed this thing? Shouldn't we be hearing all the sirens of the police responding and where are the jets to come and bomb this thing? Before I had the chance to reconcile any of those thoughts, I heard Dave, who was now sitting with half his body out the window of the car announced that it had begun moving again. We all rolled down our windows and stuck our heads out trying to get a good look. The blinking lights on the bottom of the ship were still blinking brightly and they cruised along the night sky, blocking the stars from view along its path. As I peered my eyes towards the horizon, trying to determine where it would go next, I caught sight of the most obvious choice. I could see the bright white lights of the football stadium, where our school was currently battling our local rivals.

"It's heading for the football game!" proclaimed Chuck.

"I'm on it," I said without hesitation.

I quickly threw the car into drive and shoved the gas pedal back to the ground again. My rear-wheel-drive sent the tires into a burnout, and the car's back end began to move sideways before finally propelling us forward. I genuinely wasn't sure how much further what little gas left in the tank would take us, but I was going to chase this thing until every last drop was gone.

We were going well above the speed limit, flying back down Main street trying to get to the football stadium as quickly as possible.

"Woooohooooo!" someone shouted from the backseat. It was about the only thing you could hear over the revving of the engine and the wind rushing in through the open windows. Despite our high speeds and reckless effort to keep up, the UFO had already made it to the game by the time we made it to the parking lot for the school. It was still packed with cars, illuminated by the white parking lot lights and bright lights of the stadium peeking through from over the bleacher sections. As we cruised through the parking lot at a more reasonable speed, we could hear the muffled sounds of the announcer, calling the game over the loudspeakers. It was a very different sight than we expected. We fully expected to see everyone driving away in a panic, people screaming and running for their lives, thinking we were under attack from the aliens in the sky. I pictured every invasion film I had ever watched where we pull in as people are climbing over cars, children are crying for their lost parents among all the chaos. I looked back up again wondering when the laser beam was going to come out of the bottom of the ship to blow the stadium up. Come to think of it, maybe we shouldn't be getting so close after all.

There was nothing. No panic. No mass exodus of the people attending the game. No children lost or screaming. No laser beams. Just the sounds of the game, the crowd that was watching, and the feeling of a cool crisp fall night breeze, while a ship from outer space sat directly above us.

I poked my head back out the window, watching the UFO hover, not all that high above the stadium. The only movement it made was a slight sway from left to right, like it was trying to maintain its altitude and position. There were no erratic movements. Only the continuous blinking of different colored lights coming from the bottom of the massive ship. That's when it struck me. It wasn't necessarily trying to be obvious, but it definitely wasn't behaving like something that cared if it was spotted either. It was like it was hiding in plain sight.

"It's watching us," I said.

"What do you mean?" Steve asked from the passenger seat next to me. Dave and Chuck leaned in next, waiting for my explanation.

"From the moment we spotted it and while we have been chasing it, it has been focusing on well-lit areas only, just going from spot to spot. If it wanted to attack, it would have done it already. So, I think it is here just to observe us. Watch what's going on, ya know?"

No one said another word. What I said made sense and they were left to wrestle with the thought that aliens from another planet were for some reason visiting our tiny little midwestern town, and they were actively observing us as we went about our Friday night activities. We were like creatures in a zoo, and they were the scientists in their white lab coats watching us, taking notes on their clipboard from the other side of the glass. We were aware of their presence, but we didn't truly understand who or what they were.

Dave shouted, "It's moving again! Like, fast!"

I spun my head back up towards the sky and he was right. It was heading further away from town and it had definitely picked up its pace again. I looked back down at my dashboards to see the needle for my gas level pointing directly at the E.

"As long as we keep somewhat close to it and it doesn't go too far across town, the next time it stops, we'll pull into a gas station and fill up. That way we can keep chasing it until something happens." My plan seemed like a good idea, but it was dependent on the UFO hopefully stopping and not going too far, despite it picking up speed quite a bit compared to its previous movements, but what else were we supposed to do?

"Sounds good to me," Steve said. Everyone nodded their heads and off we went again.

As I pulled back onto Main street, watching the lights of the football stadium get smaller and more distant behind us in my side view mirror, we all began to realize just how much ground the UFO had gained on us. If it weren't for how big it was, we would have lost it for sure. We kept our eyes fixed on the blinking lights as we flew up and down different streets, desperately trying to gain back some of the ground we had lost. Unfortunately, it seemed we no longer had luck on our side. It seemed like we were hitting every single red light there was along the way, and I could only push my luck so far after blowing several of them without getting caught. We just couldn't keep up and we were starting to lose hope.

As much as I wanted to continue the chase, we had somehow managed to drive clear into the other side of town without running out of gas and only country roads were ahead of us. If we ran out of gas beyond this point, it was going to be a long walk back to the nearest gas station and our parents would probably get worried sick about us when we didn't come home before curfew. Once we made it out a bit into a more open farming area without trees to obstruct our view, I turned the wheel, pulled over on the side of the road, and shut the car off.

"What the hell, Frank?" Chuck got angry at me for my sudden choice. I snapped my head around and glared right at him. I was just as pissed that we couldn't keep going but I knew what it meant if we did.

"Do you want to be the one that walks back into town and gets us gas when I run out?" I asked. He put his head down and scoffed. He knew I was right, but he wasn't going to admit it. "Didn't think so."

We all slowly opened our doors and emerged from the car, still looking to the sky, staring on as we watched an alien spaceship from another world hover in the distance watching the human race go about their mundane tasks. It had finally come to a stop again not far from an old historic landmark, a tall brick building with a backlit clock on it that sat on the far end of the city. Even if we drove there as quickly as we could with a full tank of gas, it would take us another 20 minutes to get there. We had lost the race.

Observing it observing us from this far away actually presented us with a unique opportunity to get a different look at the UFO from a new angle. Up until this point, due to the size of the ship and how close we were, we had been stuck staring at the bottom of the ship mostly, unable to make out any real detail about the rest of the ship. However, from this far away, we could still see all the blinking lights of the bottom, but we could also see the sides and most importantly, the top. The overall shape of the ship was straight out of every science fiction movie anyone had ever seen. It was a saucer shape, slightly rounded on the bottom and top. There were more blinking lights of different colors along the sides of the ship, but one thing that stood out the most was the very top center. It wasn't completely rounded out like the bottom. Instead, it had another domed protrusion coming out of it that was glowing a constant dark dull red color. We assumed this was like a cockpit area where our observers watched us from their seats, occasionally clicking different colored buttons or flipping switches to engage different observation instruments. I started to feel a bit uneasy about the whole thing. Thinking of the cockpit and aliens watching us overwhelmed my mind a bit too much and made the reality of what we were witnessing feel a little too real.

"What do we do now?" Steve asked everyone.

We had been sitting on the side of the dark, old worn-down country road for around 10 minutes now. Some of us were leaning against the car while others just stood there in the middle of the road, not worried about traffic coming by often in this area, all of us, heads tilted towards the sky, waiting for what would happen next. A long moment of silence passed before anyone spoke up to answer Steve's question.

Dave finally said, "I think we just watch, man. This is unreal. Is this even really happening right now?"

"Yeah………..it is," Chuck responded.

I wasn't much in the mood to talk at this point anymore. For me, something had shifted. There was more of a breeze as some of the taller grass surrounding the farms near us swayed with the change in the wind. The air itself felt electric and it was like I could feel or sense that something was about to happen. I kept my eye firmly planted, watching the ship as everyone else conversed.

Suddenly, it began to move again, ever so slightly. Then, little by little, the ship formed a white glow around it, which continued getting brighter and brighter with each passing second. This was it. I wasn't sure what was about to happen, but something was definitely going to happen, good or bad yet to be determined. The red dull glow of the cockpit and all the other blinking lights gave way to the bright white light and just as it got so bright that I thought it might explode, it shot like a bullet straight up into the sky. I barely had time to blink before it was completely out of sight. Gone without a trace. My mind was blown. There wasn't a cloud in the sky. The stars were shining bright as ever. This thing shot up so fast that we lost sight of it into nothing other than the darkness of space itself. I can't even begin to imagine how fast it must have been going. Imagine watching a plane go across the sky. You can watch those sometimes for several minutes before they are too far away to see anymore. This ship accomplished the same effect within less than a single second.

"Where did it go?"

"Is it gone?"

"Woah, duuuuuuuuude."

Everyone stood around trying to comprehend what they just witnessed, but I stayed silent. My eyes continued to scan every single inch of the night sky, frantically searching for a place where it may come back down. However, as more and more time passed with nothing happening and no sign of the ship coming back it became clear. That was it. It was gone.

"Nooooow what do we do?" Steve said, this time with a hint of sarcasm, acknowledging the fact that the mood in the group had shifted slightly.

No one answered. We all just got back in the car and began one of the most silent, awkward drives any of us had ever experienced. Where do you go from here? Not even an hour ago, we were desperately trying to find something to do while I shook down my cousin for a few dollars to fill up my now very empty tank. Honestly, it was probably running on fumes at this point. Then, next thing you know, we are chasing a freaking UFO all over town before watching it disappear into the sky without a trace. I went from honestly thinking the world might be ending, back to a boring Friday night in an instant. We were back to square one. It was a dejection on a level I hadn't really experienced before.

I finally stopped to get gas. As I popped the tank, grabbing the nozzle from the pump, Chuck got out of the car saying he needed some fresh air. I couldn't blame him. We were all trying to reconcile in our minds what we had just witnessed. It didn't take long to put $3 worth of gas in the car, although it did fill-er-up to more than half a tank. Then we got on the road again.

"Seriously, guys....... what do we do now?" Steve was being serious this time.

"I think I just want to go home," said Chuck. He was definitely the most shaken out of us.

"Not a bad idea. It's only downhill from here." Dave responded.

"Fine by me." Steve chimed in. "What about you, Frank? You okay?"

"Yeah, I'm fine. I agree with you guys. Not much else to do tonight."

I dropped everyone off one by one. The rides in between continued to be silent while we all were a bit distracted with our own inner thoughts. After I got everyone else safely to their houses, I returned home, eyes half on the road and half up to the sky, hoping the UFO would somehow return if I wished for it hard enough.

I walked into my house and was greeted by both my parents sitting on the couch, watching T.V. "How was your night, honey?" my mom asked me in that cheerful way only a mom can do when greeting their child. I didn't dare tell my parents what we saw or give any hint that I had broken every single rule of the road that exists. "It was good. Just kind of a boring night, so we called it early." I figured keeping it short and sweet was my best option to avoid having to lie too much. I quickly scurried up to my room to prevent any further conversation from being had.

I laid awake in my bed; curtains open looking out the window lost in thought as the light of the moon shown into my room. Maybe that's where they went. Who knows? I was stuck tossing and turning unable to figure out or make sense of everything that had happened. I attempted to think of logical explanations for what we might have witnessed, but my eyes had seen what my eyes had seen. All the things I could come up with, like an air balloon or an airplane didn't fit the description for what we saw. In fact, everyone with me agreed that it was an alien spaceship. We spent a lot of time observing it, in the same way that it was observing us. I know what I saw and that's that. But why did it come here? What was their purpose? I rolled over, finally feeling tired enough to maybe get an hour of sleep or so. The sun began to rise as I slowly drifted off, probably dreaming of aliens in my sleep.

I woke up in the morning and went down to have breakfast. I was tired and not in the best of moods. As I sat down at the table, my dad had just finished reading the paper and threw it over to me. "Take a look at this," he said, pointing to an article saying that tons of reports had been made of a flying saucer or UFO the night before near our home. "If you'd have seen that, bet you wouldn't have been so bored last night, right?" he said with a slight chuckle under his breath. He couldn't even begin to imagine.

I quickly picked up the paper, reading at a furious pace. It was exactly what we saw. All of the reports matched up. They even had a little map of where there had been different sightings, which followed the path we witnessed the UFO take. Validation at last! However, as I continued reading, I noticed that the article went on to include a statement from the local military base located just on the edge of town.

> "*On the night of October, the 5th, the United States Army and The United States Airforce conducted a joint operation to test a classified covert aircraft, which may resemble a helicopter. Our test was conducted over the course of 90 minutes and directly corresponds to the reports of an object being seen over the city. We apologize for any confusion this may have caused, but there is no need for concern among the general public. These tests help to provide valuable feedback for the United States Military. However, in the future, they will be conducted in a manner that will be less disruptive to the general public.......*"

BULLSHIT.

Not a chance. I hardly slept a wink last night trying to think about what this could have been. Are they trying to tell us that they tested a helicopter that was as big as 4 houses, and doesn't make a sound? Did they actually think we were that stupid? Also, if they are trying to do covert testing, why would they fly above so many populous areas and sit still for everyone to see? Not much of a covert test, is it? This was the dumbest thing I had ever heard, but on the other hand, it did validate that we saw something we weren't meant to see and even the military was going out of its way to cover it up.

When I went back to school on Monday, I talked with all the guys who were with me, including a few other friends. I wasn't shy about telling people what we saw, and Steve seemed on board, but Chuck and Dave wanted nothing to do with it. Apparently saying that you chased aliens on homecoming weekend instead of going to Homecoming is not good for popularity. Screw 'em. I didn't care. Plus, it was in the paper. There were thousands of people who saw this. They were turning a blind eye to the truth.

As Steve and I told another group of people what we had seen, a mutual friend of ours came up to us and told us his story. He was at the game when everything happened. Apparently, the game was a close one and the score was tied. Everyone was on the edge of their seat as our team drove the ball down the field. With only a few minutes remaining, a potential game-winning pass was thrown into the endzone, but the receiver dropped it. He said he put his hands on his head in disappointment and looked towards the sky, frustrated over the missed opportunity, but when he looked up, he spotted the huge object just sitting there above the stadium.

He recalled all the same features that we did. After having what he described as a mild panic attack, he did his best to get his friends to look up too, but their eyes were glued to the game. It doesn't help that in our friend group, he is known to be a bit of a prankster and they thought he was messing with them, maybe trying to make them miss the last few seconds of the game or something. After his failed attempt to get everyone to look he said it began moving away, quickly going out of sight. Much like Chuck, he seemed a bit shaken up over the whole thing. He told us it was nice to hear that someone else saw it because he thought he may be the only one. Although he wasn't ready to say aliens when we questioned him further, he was sure of one thing. It wasn't a group of helicopters.

In all, we never really got to the bottom of the mystery. The paper never followed up and the trail went cold. I looked towards the sky each night but saw nothing. It oddly seemed like the rest of the town blindly accepted the military's explanation, but I have never excepted it. Not to mention, it has been more than 40 years since this happened and I still have yet to see this technology of silent 4-house-wide helicopters in use; or maybe the military finally figured out how to be a bit more covert going forward. Either way, I know what I saw. I know that aliens exist. I know this because I chased one.

Reflection

I still have yet to think of any viable explanation for what we saw. It is a bit difficult to make sense of something so nonsensical. I often wonder why they came here. There really isn't much to see around this area. Were there actually hundreds or thousands of them spread out and this was just one of many? Was it like a tourist attraction or something as they were passing through our galaxy? Maybe it was an alien version of a safari or something?

I am still friends to this day with all the other guys I was with. Steve remembers and still talks about it occasionally, but that's about it. The other guys always dismiss it for some reason, still hanging on to the idea that it is weird to talk about, perhaps too concerned that people will think we are crazy.

I genuinely thought that this was not going to be a one-time experience in my life. I assumed if they had come once, they would be back again, and I would be waiting to chase them down once again. I spent a large portion of my younger years looking to the sky waiting, for that day to come, but it never did. I've never experienced anything like this again in my life, although I have plenty of years left in me, so there is still a chance. In my retirement, I go down to Arizona quite often, which for whatever reason seems to have plenty of UFO sightings and I always keep my eyes peeled. Honestly, it is a bit frustrating to know that something is out there, but I haven't been able to see it again.

Witnessing everything that we did that day hasn't really affected how I live my life too much. In my younger years, I was always the type of guy who let things roll off his shoulder. I accepted whatever happened for what it was. In this case, it just proved to me that aliens exist, and that became part of my understanding of the world we live in. When it comes down to it, I don't really care who believes me. I know what I saw, and I will keep looking up as long as I can, waiting for the day I get to hopefully see it again.

A GOOD LIFE

<u>Tony</u>

It was a good life. Filled with ups and downs, but all the events that occurred over my many years made everything worth it. The real story to tell here is the very beginning. The part of my life that set everything in motion and led me to where I am now.

I was the first in my family to be born in the United States. I lived with my parents and 2 older brothers that were all born in Italy. Italy was a vastly different place back in the early 1900s compared to what it is now. With the unification of Italy as one state, the north maintained its long-running wealth, but the south, formerly known as the Kingdom of Two Sicily's, remained in constant poverty. Our family was from the latter and much like many other Italians of the time, my parents immigrated to the U.S. in hope of opportunity and a better life, desperately trying to escape seemingly never-ending poverty and starvation.

Despite being the land of opportunity, our life in the U.S. continued to be exceedingly difficult. We were incredibly poor, and our living conditions could never even be imagined by most people. The hardship extended far beyond just the financial. Although I was too young to remember, my parents apparently never really got along. According to both sides of the family, my mother was the root cause of the dissatisfaction. She was mostly known to be a very cold and distant person. Praise was rare, although cherished when received from her. She never held back her tongue and was always ready to speak her mind. My father on the other hand was the polar opposite. He was tall, handsome, and charming to everyone. He was universally loved and was known for going out of his way to help others, no matter how tired he was from long days of hard work, and no matter how hungry he was from lack of food being put on the table. He spared food when we didn't have any to spare. He spared change when there was none to give. I've thought for many hours during my life, trying to figure out what brought them together, wondering if my mother was different before I knew her, but I sadly never got the answers to this.

Regardless of our situation, the one thing that gave us hope was being in America. From what I was told, my family was brave. We were willing to immigrate during incredibly tough times, leaving family behind, all for an opportunity that was far from guaranteed. Truth be told, the decision to leave Italy was far from unanimous. It was my father's insistence and persuasion that sealed the deal. He essentially charmed his way across the ocean. He was convinced that there was more for us in the States. My mother, knowing she couldn't actually refuse, reluctantly went along with the plan. However, this put an even larger strain on their relationship. By the time I was 2 years old, my parents were more distant than ever before. Whatever love they once had for each other was gone and their situation became more of an exercise in tolerance than anything else. Divorce in this day, especially among Catholic Italians, was nearly unheard of, so they were stuck. At least that's what everyone thought.

My father, however, had other ideas. He knew my mother was seemingly inescapable and would never let him leave. Not a chance. Not only had he forced them here, making their lives more miserable than ever, but this would leave her with nothing, and she wouldn't allow it. He may have charmed his way to the U.S.A., but he wasn't charming his way out of their marriage. What no one ever expected though, is how prepared he was to take drastic measures if necessary, to get away from his current predicament. Evidently, no one had truly taken notice of how big a toll the move, the lack of work, and the failed marriage had on him. He had become a shell of the charming, charismatic man he used to be. Family and friends watched him slowly lose all those little quirks of his that made him who he was. He had developed a short-fuse temper. He was losing weight at an unhealthy pace. The land of opportunity had become nothing more than a bleak black and white reality in a world full of color.

My brothers recalled to me the day it all happened. The day our father snapped. Our mother was away, visiting another Italian family in the area. Our father knew she would be gone for hours and shortly after she left, he sprung to action, frantically packing all of our belongings that could fit into a single suitcase. It was like he had rehearsed this a thousand times. He was incredibly efficient. He moved between rooms with purpose, making a B-line for a particular drawer that contained something he intended on packing up. It was like watching a perfectly played game of Tetris as each item he grabbed had its own designated spot in the suitcase, slowly filling it to the top, level with the zipper. After only around 30 minutes, he closed the suitcase and turned to us.

"What's going on, Dad?" my oldest brother asked. My father stared at him for a little while. He reached out, placing both hands on each of my brother's shoulders.

"We're leaving. One day, you'll understand." Our father picked up the suitcase, got us all ready, and walked out the door with all three children along with him and never looked back.

We were essentially marched to the local train station as my brothers took turns carrying me and we all boarded with pre-purchased tickets. No one had any idea where we were being taken, and it isn't like we would have had a say in the matter anyway. It was becoming clear that this was a very well thought out plan made by our father. It felt like we were part of a movie where the secret agent is told that at a moment's notice they may need to disappear. The only problem was we didn't want to disappear, but our father decided to make the decision of going with him for us. This was kidnapping. Plain and simple.

Within a few hours, the train began to slow down, whistling its way into the station as we arrived in Chicago. After gathering what little belongings we had, we took a short ride over to the Port of Chicago. Upon arrival, staring at the substantially sized, yet rather run-down ship, my oldest brother recalled that that was when he knew we were going back home. Well, their home, not mine. We were bound for Italy.

By this time, it was likely that our mother had just returned home and realized something was very wrong. I have often visualized her face, slowly transitioning between emotions of fear, anger, and complete and utter sadness as she walked through the door, horrified to find out that her husband had left her and worse yet, taken her children with. She was most likely sitting at the kitchen table, looking at the only family photo we left behind, crying and trying to make sense of her world that had just been shattered. Our father's actions were cruelty at its finest. She had been abandoned by the few people she knew. The people she loved. We were barely making it by on my father's wages, but now she wouldn't even have that to rely on. We had left her completely alone, with nothing.

I remember thinking back many times during my life, what that must have been like. Women like her, along with women generations before her, were faced with an unthinkable choice. She was an unskilled immigrant woman who found herself without any form of financial support yet needed a way to provide for herself. So, she did what she had to do to survive. When faced with unthinkable choices, one must do the unthinkable.

One of my brothers carried me off the boat as we arrived in Italy a few weeks later. We immediately sought out the remaining family of our father to stay with. No one knew we were coming. I can only imagine their shock when their cousin and his three children showed up at their door. My father had kept his plans a secret from everyone. He thought it was too risky to let anyone know since it could put his plan in jeopardy. Nothing was stopping him from making his decision.

Thankfully, Italians living in this era were resourceful by nature; surviving on very little was something they knew all too well. Even though they were probably biting off more than they could chew, we were welcomed with open arms and taken care of temporarily while my father searched for work. All the favors he had done for so many years began to pay off, and people were eager to help him for once. The idea of paying off debt is a big thing in Italian culture. No matter how big or small a favor is, you now owe them and will go to great lengths to pay it off. Accepting a grown man and his three children into your home unexpectedly, feeding them, and taking care of them was like hitting the lottery of paying off favors.

It didn't take long for our father to get a job and start receiving a steady income. It also helped that he was quite the handyman and was good at doing whatever task he was faced with. Not only could he charm his way into anything, but he also typically had the means to put his money where his mouth was. Being handy is one of the things he would pass on to me. I loved to tinker with stuff and figure out how it worked. In a different life, I should have been an engineer. The skills passed on to me would serve me well and translated into a multitude of working skills later in my life to get me through the hardest years.

My father continued to save up the money he was making and after a while, we got a home with a small plot of farmable land to help us provide for ourselves. Much to our surprise, our father quickly remarried, although he was never really divorced. As the days passed, the changes we had already noticed in him back in the U.S. began to become more prominent. His demeanor shifted. He lost the charm completely, hardly even so much as smiling, and he became incredibly selfish. I would watch as he dressed in his best suit only to go sit on the front porch of our home and look on while my brother and his new wife did grueling work in the farm fields. He became so self-important. His focus was geared only towards himself and occasionally us children. But the worst part was that he pretended like the life he had before didn't exist anymore. When he spoke of the past, he never went further back than the day we arrived in Italy. He disconnected from his former life completely. I would ask questions about the United States and my mother, only to be ignored. I worried about her, but my father never spoke of her again.

My frustration with his behavior grew to hatred and resentment. Not only was he turning into something no one liked, but I couldn't forget what he had done to us. What he had made of our lives. By all means, he had done well for us since coming back to Italy. Surprisingly, our life was better than it ever was before and even better than in the U.S., but it was not the life I wanted. I didn't ask for this. It was forced on me against my will. This was not my home, and I didn't belong here. I belonged with our mother in the home where I was born. People in Italy still spoke of the U.S. as being the place to go. Our neighbors and people in surrounding towns still left each day in search of other opportunities. I dreamed of going back, but as young as I was, I never stood a chance, so I continued to just try to survive. I kept my head down and continued to press forward, dreaming of the day I could go home.

As the years went by, our living conditions and our relationship only got worse. The 1st World War had begun, which acted as a stark reminder of how difficult surviving can be. The already terribly poor and starving people of Sicily became poorer and hungrier than ever before. I hated everything about my life at this point. I was forced to work in the fields every moment I wasn't being forced to go to school. My origins as a U.S. citizen had to be kept very quiet. I was the dirty secret of the family that didn't belong. If anyone found out, we could have been run out of town or worse. I could be killed. Before the Italian's finally entered the war, we were not part of the Allies. It was only found out later that during secret talks Italy switched sides to join the Allies. Regardless of the decisions made by the country, not everyone around us agreed with the direction leadership was taking and it remained best to keep my birth origin a secret.

All of this made me so angry. I began going out of my way to make my father's life as difficult as possible. If he wanted me to do something, I did the opposite. If he wished for me to learn, I would actively forget. He always told me he wanted me to grow up to be a strong and healthy man, so I began smoking at the age of 7, and I didn't quit until I was 70! I started going out of my way to become the troublesome kid in school. I knew education was immensely important to my father. He was never educated properly and therefore he wanted to make sure at least one of his kids got the chance to learn the things he never did. I became a complete hellion in school to spite my father's wishes. After so many pranks and attempts at getting kicked out of school, I finally got what I wanted.

One of our teachers would always fall asleep at his desk while we did our classwork. He was old and mostly bald, with hair only growing around the sides of his head connecting to the long white beard that went halfway down his chest. He always sat at the front, reading our schoolwork, stroking his beard, and mumbling in Italian until he dozed off. One day, during a particularly boring lesson, he fell asleep sitting up, chin resting on his chest, and his hands clasped across his belly. I convinced a classmate to be my accomplice and we quietly snuck up to his desk, much to the horror of the rest of the classroom. I could feel their gazing eyes, begging me not to pull yet another prank on the teacher. Oftentimes, my antics got the entire class in trouble. Guilty by association I think, but I didn't care. This was payback for my father's actions against me, and the rest of my class was just collateral damage.

I took one of the matches I kept around for my smoking habit from my pocket. We carefully lit the match and placed it against his beard that was resting nicely across his chest and over his clasped hands. Once it lit, we tried to do our best to get back to our desks and act like nothing had happened. This didn't go as planned. For some unknown reason, our teacher's beard was very flammable, and it went up in flames immediately. The stench of burnt hair quickly filled the room, and we made it no more than three steps from his desk when he woke in a panic. He frantically stood up, knocking his chair out from under his legs. His back slammed against the chalkboard, smearing that day's lesson into a blur of white and he hit his beard repeatedly, trying to knock out the flames while yelling every single profanity in Italian that he could muster. We looked on, never imagining that this would be the result of our actions. Once the flames were extinguished, we knew we had done it this time. Our teacher didn't say a word as he walked towards us, his beard only half of what it used to be, the ends now blackened and burnt as he grabbed both of us by the collars and literally threw us out the door, telling us never to return. That was the last day of school I ever attended.

From that point on, I was told to pull my weight since I was being such a burden and was forced to work in the fields on the farm, day in and day out. It was long grueling hours of manual labor. With each digging action of my shovel, I would drift off in thought, still dreaming of being home in the states, eating a home-cooked Italian meal with my mother. I wanted this more than anything.

After the war ended, life started to change as Mussolini came to power. I hate to admit this now, but to the Sicilians like us, he was nothing short of a God. We were uneducated and poor, but under his reign we had pensions, and we were actually paid for work performed. For the first time in my life, and certainly most Italian's lives, we felt like we were going to be taken care of. We were finally being put first rather than being an afterthought. At some point, not long after coming to power, Mussolini came to a neighboring town, and we took the chance to go see him in person. As he walked through the crowd, he came right towards me. I just about damn near froze in my tracks as he reached his hand out to shake mine. The next thing I knew, at 14 years old, I was shaking hands with one of the worst dictators to have ever lived. I used to think of this as a bragging point, but I can look back at it now and understand how short-sighted this all was. The veil was still over our eyes. We were all so unaware of what he was really doing. News was only good because he had the means to suppress the bad, and those who opposed him never opposed for long.

Thankfully, I saw through this before most. As I watched those around me praise him, I recognized that nothing was actually different. It was a false sense of security and only furthered my feeling of not belonging. I saw that the poor were still poor, the hungry were still hungry and nothing was going to change that. I wasn't fooled by the promises of better days. I knew that they would not come, at least not any time soon, and things would probably only get much worse before they ever got better.

So, at the age of 17 years old, I took a page out of my father's book and I made a plan. I was going to undo everything he did to me. I no longer wanted to follow if he was going to be my leader. I was going back to the U.S., back to my home, and nothing could stop me. I knew the risks. This was not going to be easy, and my life was going to get much harder before it became any easier, but at least I could face those difficulties somewhere I felt like I belonged.

First things first, I needed to find my mother. All I knew was her name. I put some feelers out there to people I trusted and before I knew it, I had a location. Chicago. Apparently, a few old friends of my family had still occasionally kept in touch with her via letters over the years. I didn't tell them why I wanted the information, and they didn't ask. I made sure to give them a few vegetables from our field to repay them for the favor and my debt to them was now paid.

Immigrating was difficult even if you were financially stable, but I was choosing to do it with nothing.

However, I believed firmly that I could accomplish what my father could not. Besides, if I really break it down, I wasn't technically immigrating, I was going back home. For the first time in my life, my U.S. citizenship wasn't a burden, and it would make getting where I was going a little bit easier.

I feel guilty about this next part, but I snuck into my brother's belongings and stole the money necessary to get me where I needed to go. I wasn't paid to work in the fields, so I was doing what I had to. When the time came and I felt ready to pull the trigger, I quietly packed up what little belongings I had and laid out my one and only suit to wear on the journey home. I stood there in my room, looking around at the plain brown wooden walls and I felt no comfort, no longing, no loss. These four walls felt more like a prison to me than a home. It was time to go.

In the early hours of the morning before anyone else had risen, I quietly put on my suit, organized what little items I was bringing with, and mentally prepared myself to leave, running through my internal checklist of things I needed to have to make sure this all worked. I hadn't told a soul. I felt guilty about leaving my brothers in the dark on this, but I don't believe for one second they would have come with, and their loyalty to my father would certainly lead them to rat me out. I was in this alone. I tip-toed my way out of the house, into the still dark morning, and turned around to look back at where I had spent the last 15 years of my life. I examined it, the old and warped windows, rotting wood starting to fall and the rocking chair on the front porch where my father loved to sit, ordering everyone around. I took it all in before I turned my head, looking down the street, barely lit by the light of the moon, and began my journey home, never looking back.

I made it to the train station before the sun even rose and stood on the platform, mostly alone. The train rolled in and I handed the worker my ticket and boarded. I sat at the window, watching the fields pass as the sun slowly breached over the horizon. It was the first time I felt at peace in a very long time.

The trip across the ocean ended up taking several weeks and was filled with a few bouts of bad weather. We arrived at Ellis Island, where I went through customs and my name is still searchable in the Library of Congress along with the other 22 million people that came through there over the years. All of my careful planning was working out rather well until this very moment. I had used nearly every bit of money I had to buy the tickets and get to the United States. Now, the amount remaining was needed to get on a train to Chicago, where I would start having to ask around to find where my mother was living at the time. I rationed everything from this point, surviving on only the absolute bare minimum required to stay alive. I was used to hunger, so it didn't bother me like it probably would most.

Upon my arrival in Chicago, I hopped off the train and wasn't too sure of what to do next. No one knew I was coming. No one even knew who I was, so I did the only thing I could do and started asking random people on the streets if they knew my mother. I must have asked thousands of people each day, standing there on the corner, wandering the alleyways, sleeping on a bench at night still dressed in my only suit. Finally, I came across a man that recognized her name. He gave me the address and I thanked him endlessly as he waved goodbye wishing me luck in my journey.

After a few more hours of walking to the address I was given, I arrived, feet swollen, cheeks sunken from hunger, and sleep-deprived at the front door of where I was told my mother lived. I cautiously walked up the stoop to the front door and knocked three times. I heard footsteps approaching the door, followed by a latch being undone and the handle turning as the door opened and I was greeted by a short little Italian woman. She barely stood at five feet tall and was just about as big around. She had curly short black hair and was wearing what looked to be a homemade cotton house dress with an apron on over it.

"Hello?" she said as she looked at me like a stranger. I took a step back. I never really prepared myself for this moment. I never thought to consider that she wouldn't recognize me. I was a child the last time she saw me and now here I was, a grown man standing before her. "Hi, Mom," I said calmly as I nervously placed my hands in my pockets, tilting my head down, still trying to look up and see her reaction. There was a long pause as her face came to life and her eyes widened. She placed her hands to her mouth and took a deep breath realizing what I had just said.

"Tony? Oh, Tony! Is that you? Oh, my baby boy, is that you?" she lunged herself at me, hugging me tightly, and began to cry. "Oh, my goodness, I have missed you so much. My baby boy, you've grown up to be so big!"

She took a step back from me, keeping her hands on my cheeks as she smiled, her head slightly tilted and looked me in the eyes. She was truly happy. She turned around gesturing with her hands, "Come in, come in!"

I was home. I was finally home.

As I walked into her home, I took a moment to look around as many of my fears growing up thinking about her were coming to life. The house was falling apart, paint peeling from the walls, cabinets barely hanging to the walls and very little of the carpet, probably original to the home, was left on the floor leaving only the exposed wood to walk on. Her life had clearly been harder than I ever could have imagined. She was living in complete poverty. My jaw clenched as I tightened my fist at my side, setting down my suitcase, standing there in the entryway to the home. This was my father's doing. How could he? How could he have done something like this to the woman he claimed to have once loved?

She sat me down in a wobbly chair at the kitchen table, which barely held itself up by the four legs it was standing on. She turned, still wearing a smile from ear to ear and a little more pep in her step, and walked to the kitchen to grab some cookware out of the cupboards. It wasn't long until the water was boiling, and the air was filled with the smells of pasta and spices. She brought back out two plates, one for her and one for me, filled to the brim with pasta. For the first time in my life that I could remember, I sat at the kitchen table with my mother, eating a home-cooked Italian meal made with love, the way only an Italian mother can make it.

Some time passed and I slowly got settled into my new home and new way of living. It became clear to me how my mother survived all this time. Unthinkable choices. As I sat around for a few days, taking a break from the constant chaos my life had been up to this point, I never bothered to get to know all the men that came around, renting a room or two by the hour or however long was needed as my mother or another mistress kept them "company."

I brushed those thoughts from my head as my mother and I would sit and talk, catching up on what life was like for me in Italy and I also had to get through the difficult conversation that I was the only one who came back. My mother used some of her connections to get me a job at a local warehouse doing manual labor, something I had become very good at through the years in the fields. As I started making a little money, I used it to help her fix the home up, little by little.

As I worked my new 9 to 5, some other Italians in the warehouse started to smell blood in the water. It didn't take long before I was approached about a new and interesting opportunity. The guy who approached me noticed that during inventory counting, I was decent with numbers and thought I might make for a good bookkeeper in his organization. It wasn't hard to figure out what his organization was. The Italian Mafia in Chicago at the time was infamous. Even I had heard rumors of them back in my little rural farming village in Italy. My mother had already warned me this would happen, and she urged me against it. Apparently, only a few weeks before, a friend of hers had a son who was killed not long after taking a job like this. For all I knew, I was his replacement. I was told he was on his way to work one day and the next thing he knew, he was surrounded by guys who opened fire in broad daylight.

I told my mother about the offer after getting home from work that day. It was the only time I ever saw her so angry she began throwing things, breaking them against the wall. "Not my son!" she yelled. She knew this was most likely a smaller part of Capone's operation, a name that at the time was just beginning to become known within the city. Furthermore, she knew it was most likely a death sentence for me. I went to work and politely turned down the position along with the 20 or so other offers that followed for months afterward until they finally gave up on me.

From those days on, I did my best to keep my head down and avoid being noticed. Making an honest living was very difficult. Italians weren't treated the best in the U.S., but it didn't bother me too much. I knew this wasn't going to be easy from the beginning. I occasionally thought about what I left behind in Italy. I never missed it, not even for a moment, but it still made me sad that my father, nor either of my brothers, had bothered to reach out to me after I left despite me contacting them, letting them know what I did and where I was. I was unsure if I would ever hear from them again. I always knew it was a possibility, but knowing it was possible and actually experiencing it are very different things.

Living in the U.S.A. turned out to be better than I could have ever imagined. I did all the things I never bothered to do back in Italy. I never got close to anyone before because I had to be so careful about my citizenship. I finally wasn't some dirty little secret to be swept under the rug and not discussed. I met new friends. We went to movies and dinners. I finally felt like I was home.

Eventually, I even managed to muster the courage to ask someone out who would become the future love of my life. Nancy was the most amazing woman I had ever met. She was so strong-willed and fierce, yet calm and kind. On our first date, her family didn't trust me, so when we went to a movie the entire family came along, too. I was sat at one end on the aisle next to her father, and she sat next to her mother on the opposite end with all of her brothers and sisters in between. Sooner or later, I finally earned the family's trust and after about a year of seeing one another, we got married and began what would become the most wonderful 76 years of my life. She made the hard times easier and the best times even better. Despite our old Italian bickering as we sat in our rocking chairs throughout our later years, I somehow managed to love her more every single day.

After meeting Nancy, I finally felt like I was doing what I was supposed to do. I was where I wanted to be. Like I said, life by no means was easy for an Italian immigrant who had spent most of his early years working the fields in Sicily. However, if it gave me anything, it gave me grit and stubbornness matched by few.

We moved to a neighboring city to settle down and start a family but never stopped visiting families in Chicago every single Sunday. Unfortunately, the struggles life throws at you were not done. Not long after we married, the markets crashed, followed by what would become known as the Great Depression. These times were tougher than any other before. Nancy became pregnant with our first child, a baby boy, and we were barely getting by. I did what had to be done, no matter what. I even went door to door, offering the skills I had for what little pay could be offered. I made deals with the local grocery store that when something needed fixing, they would find me, and I accepted food as payment for my work. At one point, I took a job cutting back some large trees. As I cut a larger branch away, it fell to the ground and chopped the ladder out from under me, causing me to fall about 15 feet. The large pile of branches broke both my fall and my back. It put me out of work for months. It made the bills higher than they already were, right as we brought a child into the world. I was left with no choice, and through sheer will, far before the doctor said I was supposed to, I returned to work. I was not going to fail my family. I refused to give up when things got hard. That was what my father did, and I was going to be nothing like him. I got back to work and kept pushing forward.

Thankfully, with a little bit of luck and a whole lot of hard work, I managed to get a job with a local manufacturer near where I lived. It provided the steady income we needed to get us through the toughest of times. I vowed that my family would never know the struggles that I did while I worked endlessly to give them the best life possible. Nancy soon became pregnant again, this time with a little girl. For 40 more years, I would work to give them everything. In fact, my daughter would grow up often mad at me for doing too much. She complained that because I always took care of everything, she never got to learn how to do it. She never learned how to cook all of Nancy's recipes or how to fix the washing machine when it made the clunking sound that it sometimes did. Perhaps she was right, but it was a small price to pay for having the life that I was never given.

My life was everything I wanted it to be, for me, my wife, and my children. There was only one thing left to do. Something I refused to do up to this point. I looked back. I wasn't sure if I was ever going to do anything with the information, but a few years prior I tracked down my brothers in Italy. Surprisingly, they finally wrote me back. I learned my father had passed away long before this point, I wasn't interested in a relationship with him anyway, but my brothers were everything to me as a child.

In 1976, I decided to make the trip back to Italy to do my best to unite my family. It was truly one of the most wonderful trips I had ever made. We crammed 50 years of life into a weeklong trip, staying up all hours of the night, smoking cigars, drinking coffee, eating my favorite biscotti cookies, and talking about days gone by. It finally gave me closure on a chapter of my life that had been left open for far too long. This trip had that last hurrah type of feel. We kept in touch after my return home, but as time passed, the letters came and went less frequently. Eventually, the day would come twice, when a letter from family I didn't even know came, informing me of my brother's passing.

My life continued to take many twists and turns after these years, filled with many surprises. The tiny child that had been kidnapped and sent to Italy against his will, finally grew up. In all, I have lived to see 6 wars and 17 presidents. I even became the President of my city's local Democratic party. In stark contrast to my former handshake in Italy, this actually gave me the opportunity to shake hands with JFK himself when he visited our town while running for President of the United States. At one point not long after, I found myself being groomed to potentially run for the mayor's office. However, I turned the chance down since I didn't feel like I had the proper education to be the Mayor. I do hope my childhood teacher was eventually able to grow his beard back.

For the first time in my life, no matter where I was, I felt love. I had learned to forgive and the resentment was gone as all my hard work, persistence, and grit had paid off. My children had children of their own, who had their own children too. Starting from the fields of Italy making it all the way to my rocking chair today, sitting next to the love of my life, it was all worth it. The struggle, the pain, the joy, and the pleasure. Every last bit of it. It was a good life.

Reflection

The narrator of this story sadly passed away in 2004. However, as he mentioned when telling his story, he had plenty of family that survived beyond him. His Great Grandson was more than happy to reflect in any way he could on his behalf stating, "I am happy to share his amazing life with others. He was the rock of our family and an inspiration to many as he passed down so many values throughout the multiple generations of our family."

I can honestly say that I have never come across someone quite like him again in my life. He had always dropped hints throughout my childhood of the kind of life he had lived. Through my naivety and obliviousness, however, I unfortunately never prompted him to explain more. At one point, my father, who knew him much better than I, told me that I should sit down with my Great Grandfather and get to know him better. He basically suggested I interview him. I was 14 years old or so and couldn't really understand why this was so necessary. I was such an ignorant kid. As I spoke with him, he sat there, probably excited and willing to answer anything I asked. Maybe he even hoped he would finally get to pass on his story to me. Instead, I asked nothing more than a few basic questions, that I only wrote down half answers to on a piece of paper that I later threw away.

What a lost opportunity, and to this day, it is something I regret immensely.

I had an opportunity to learn from a true survivor and to gain so much knowledge by speaking to him. If I could go back now, I would love to sit and listen to him speak and tell his stories for days. I would have endless questions. Thankfully, I was able to speak with the remaining living relatives to piece this story together, and I am proud to say that this is the most complete version of his life's story that exists today. Someone can learn so much by hearing the experiences of others and I only wish that he could tell this story himself.

BRASS KNUCKLES

Michelle

I didn't live in a safe part of town. I didn't work in a safe part of town either, but I couldn't get out. At this point in my life, I was working a job that didn't exactly pay the best. As much as I would have loved to get a better job and a home in a nicer area, my skills were limited and open positions in the city were few and far between. With a newborn son at home, I did what I needed to in order to get by.

In my neighborhood, being a young woman unfortunately made me stand out as a bit of a target. Although I pride myself on being in pretty good shape, that only goes so far when it comes time to defend yourself.

That's why my mom gave me her brass knuckles.

I was shocked when she handed them to me. My mother was not a person who condoned violence in any way, but I think she knew the reality of my situation. She told me that my father gave them to her a long time ago. He was a golden gloves boxer and knew how to fight, but he never managed to make a career out of it. Instead, he ended up as a janitor at the local high school, and my mother didn't really work, so he gave them to her since she was home alone so often. Something was better than nothing, I guess.

I always felt weird carrying them around in my purse. If I'm not mistaken, they are technically illegal, but who's keeping track, right? At the time, I couldn't possibly imagine what it would be like to use them. I had never been in a real fight before, only the occasional skirmish or two with my brothers. I told a couple of my close friends that I carried them around and even showed them off a few times, but everyone just poked fun at me. They said that everyone else had a gun, so unless I could dodge bullets and get in close, they would be useless. I get what they were saying, but all too often, violent acts or break-ins would occur near where I lived or worked. Every time they did, I could expect a call from my mother checking in to make sure I was okay and to ask if I still had them just in case.

The more time that went by, the more I got used to having the brass knuckles with me. It started to feel no different than carrying my wallet. Thankfully, my life maintained a pretty standard routine. I never went too far outside of my comfort zone. I couldn't really afford to. I went through each of my days the same way. Monday through Friday, I worked long hours at a job I didn't enjoy, but it paid me, and during those same weeknights, I would round up what I could to make dinner, making sure my son was well taken care of. He still wasn't sleeping through the nights so oftentimes my long days were preceded by long nights. I learned to operate in a state of utter exhaustion as many parents do. On the weekends I focused on family and tried to enjoy what little quality time we had together. I made it my mission to keep my head low and try not to screw up. Unfortunately, on one particular day, I did just that.

It was the middle of the week, and in my overly exhausted state from working too many hours while taking care of a newborn, I forgot to set an alarm. Thank goodness my mother woke me up with a phone call wondering why I hadn't yet shown up with my son. I scrambled out of the house and raced to drop him off for the day before speeding as fast as I could to work. When I got to our building, all the parking spaces were taken. The business I worked for was in a busy part of the downtown area, so I had to drive around the block looking for street parking, which I found just on the other side of a nearby park. I wasn't happy about the additional walk since it made me later than I already was.

The day went by like normal, thankfully without any additional surprises, and my boss wasn't as upset as I expected him to be. I got off work around 3pm, and it was an absolutely gorgeous summer day. The warm sun against my skin and the light breeze blowing through was truly refreshing after being cooped up in the office all day. The extra walk through the park didn't seem so bad anymore.

I couldn't have been more wrong.

Most people avoided the park since many homeless people often congregated there and were considered by the majority of the city to be lazy bums who just couldn't hold a job. I didn't share the same uncompassionate opinion though. It's just ignorance. Most people were so out of touch with the struggle others faced. They didn't see what certain areas were like before the industry that supported the city left and went overseas. So many people had been left without a job and with nowhere to go. It always hurt me to see their struggle knowing that the journey to find a way out was going to be difficult, if not impossible. It reminded me of my own struggle.

I continued my stroll through the park minding my own business and enjoying the beautiful weather. I walked past an older man with gray hair and a long gray beard. He was dressed in warmer clothes despite it being at least 70 degrees and sunny outside. His face was withered and disgruntled, undoubtedly from the hard life he'd most likely endured. He had a hat out for collecting money with a sign in front of it that read, "Any little bit helps." I honestly didn't have much to give, but if any little bit helped, I figured I would at least give him the spare change I had on me. I reached into my purse to grab my wallet, took out what I had, and dropped it into the hat. The old man didn't even flinch. He just stared forward with a glaze over his eyes. I didn't do it for a reaction, so I kept moving along, hoping that even the small sum I could spare would make a difference for him.

"I'll take some of that," said the man sitting on the bench just a few steps in front of me. I hadn't noticed him until this point. He must have been watching me give the homeless man my change because it clearly caught his attention. He wasn't too much in stature, probably a few inches taller than me, skinny and dressed in jeans and a t-shirt. He didn't fit the mold of a stereotypical homeless person. Instead, he was more than likely there because he either had nothing better to do or was up to no good. Just because you're not homeless, doesn't mean you aren't experiencing hard times. I knew this feeling all too well, and I could definitely relate to that sentiment at the time. It was pretty well known that someone desperate enough for cash was not above stealing from anyone, including the homeless, so my thoughts began racing, wondering what the intentions of this man were to me or the man I just gave money to.

He got up abruptly from his bench as I was about to walk past. I kept my head down, doing my best to ignore him.

SMACK!!!

Suddenly, all I could feel was a searing pain on the side of my face. I still don't know to this day whether he punched me or slapped me. All I know is that my cheek and ear were on fire. I stumbled off to the side and just as I was about to fall, something yanked me back up. It was the man trying to take off with my purse, but it was clinched around my arm with the strings securely in the bend of my elbow, which gave me a bit of leverage to pull back with.

He was much stronger than me. Each yank pulled me forward off my feet a bit, but I was not about to give up. It was the middle of the day and there had to be people around, so I started screaming at the top of my lungs. "HELP! SOMEONE HELP ME!!!" He let go of the purse immediately, putting his hands up as if to indicate that he wasn't doing anything. I thought that did the trick, or at least scared him enough to make him want to run, but I think he noticed the same thing I did. The only people around were the homeless, and there was no one coming to help me.

I continued to scream at the top of my lungs while taking a few steps backward, keeping my gaze locked onto him as he started to approach me again, this time with malice in his eyes. He meant to hurt me now. He was going to get my purse and belongings by any means necessary. That much was evident. Several thoughts ran through my head at that moment. Was fighting really worth it? Giving the contents of my purse up was going to be a setback, but I could get through it. What about my newborn son? He needs me, so I can't risk my life fighting over a few dollars, right? But it wasn't in my nature. I was a fighter, and despite all the logic telling me I should drop the purse and run away, I ignored it.

I reached my hands into the purse while backpedaling and felt the brass knuckles in my hand. I slipped my fingers through them and positioned them within my clenched fist while still hidden from my assailant in the purse. He was just about to grab me again. My entire body became consumed with both crippling fear and unfathomable rage. That's when I told him he could have the damn purse as I threw it at his chest. He clearly wasn't expecting me to throw it at him like this. He fumbled and dropped it on the ground, just like I had hoped he would. He quickly bent over to pick it up, pivoting to run away. However, he failed to notice me using this distraction to wind back and thrust my fist forward towards his head with every ounce of strength I had. I had never punched anyone this hard in my life before. I have definitely tried once or twice with my older brother, but I've never connected. Today, I connected perfectly. I hit him just behind his left ear, sending him face-first into the concrete.

It was such a different sound than anything I'd ever heard before. It was a deep thud compared to the sound of a slap or a punch. My hand immediately began to hurt like hell. I'm sure I probably punched in the worst way possible, but I didn't really care because it clearly got the job done. He didn't go unconscious, but he also wasn't in the mood to fight anymore, and he didn't care about the purse either. He tried to make his best, albeit very unsuccessful, attempt to get away. Since he'd hit the ground so hard and I had knocked him at least a little bit silly, the best he could do when trying to get up from his knees was to try and launch himself back to his feet like a track runner launching off the line. Each time he tried he would stumble forward onto his face as his arms and legs would give out from under him. It was as if he'd lost all coordination, which I guess is what having your bell rung by a pair of brass knuckles will do to you.

I probably should have taken my purse and ran at that point, but I was about as stubborn as they come. This man had tried to cause me harm, and he might try to do it again someday to a non-brass knuckle wearing individual. As I picked up my purse quickly from the ground, I looked to my right and saw a man in an apron running towards us at full speed. I figured it must be a worker from the bakery across the street. He must have heard me screaming or had finally noticed the ongoing struggle. I had back up now, and that was all the encouragement I needed to make sure this man thought twice before ever trying to harm someone like this again.

My assailant was finally getting his bearings and had managed to stumble a few extra feet away from me. He was still crawling on all fours, trying to sprint off his starting line. This presented a perfect opportunity. I took about three long, lunging steps, then wound my foot back and kicked him as hard as I could right where it counted from behind. Maybe I never hit my brother with a hard punch to the head like I wanted to sometimes, but I definitely knew what even a light, well-placed hit between the legs would do. I hit my target with perfect accuracy, and he let out a yelp that I thought could only come from a dog when you step on its tail. After falling back to the ground, he rolled over on his back, wincing in pain, but I wasn't done yet. I was wearing heels. Not overly pointy ones that I sometimes like to wear, but heels, nonetheless. It was only moments before the baker was going to reach us. I needed to make these last few moments count, so I raised my foot as high as I could and stomped my heels directly into his groin as many times as possible before the baker arrived.

Once the baker reached us, he quickly pulled me away from the man. The attacker was the one who needed the saving now. I remember being belligerent and just yelling every profane word I could come up with at the man while the baker tried to calm me down. The baker walked over to the man lying on the ground and told him not to move. The police had been called and were on their way. This was way before cell phones, but apparently he had one of the other bakers call 9-1-1 while he ran to come help me.

People started to gather around after finally taking notice of all the commotion. Some of them even helped the man I just beat up sit on a bench. I had managed to quickly put the brass knuckles back into my purse when no one was paying attention. The police eventually showed up, along with an ambulance, which I refused, but the thief accepted because of the hit he took to the head. Officers questioned me about what happened, and I told them I punched the guy as hard as I could, and it caused him to lose his balance. "He must have hit his head on the ground or something, officer." They believed me. They also informed me how lucky I was too.

Apparently, there were several warrants out for this man's arrest since he had committed multiple violent crimes previously, mostly targeting women like myself. There was a moment during my counterattack where I felt bad for what I was doing but being told this information quickly pushed those thoughts aside. I regretted nothing. I politely asked the remaining officers if someone would escort me to my car since I was still a bit shook up from the incident.

I drove to my mother's house to pick up my son. The moment I walked through the door she knew something was wrong. I was very late, and I had a bit of a black eye from the initial hit I took. I explained everything that happened, and I thanked her for what I originally thought was a ridiculous gift. I told her I will always keep the brass knuckles on me from that day on. Her reaction was mixed, to say the least. She was clearly concerned that her daughter had been attacked but elated that the knuckles served their purpose when they were needed most.

"This reminds me of when your father was still boxing, and he would come home looking like you right now!" she laughed through her words. "I know how to help the swelling on that eye. Let's get you cleaned up before he gets home, and you can tell him everything."

After this event occurred, the brass knuckles took on a different meaning to me altogether. They acted as a motivator for me to get out of my living situation at all costs. I would do whatever it takes. Each time I saw them resting at the bottom of my purse, I would remember this attack. In those moments, it didn't matter what job I had, I was going to be the best at it. I told myself I would work even harder to get the raise or get the promotion, building my savings little by little until I could leave it all behind.

Eventually, all of my hard work paid off. Though my life changed considerably over the years, I made a great life for me and my son. We managed to move into a decent home in a nice area. With the experience I built from working in a variety of different positions, I eventually landed a better job with a more stable, reliable income. We started to enjoy life a little more. We took vacations and I finally got the family time I always wanted. We got to experience so much that I had only dreamed of doing in my younger years. I am proud of what I accomplished despite not being dealt the best hand at the beginning. I learned that I am brave and so much stronger than anyone gave me credit for. My attacker learned that the hard way.

Thankfully, nothing like this ever happened to me again, but I still held onto those knuckles to remember the time I beat the ever-loving snot out of the guy who tried to rob me.

Reflection

Unfortunately, the narrator of this story passed away unexpectedly during the writing of this book and was unable to give a proper reflection. However, her son has decided to reflect from his point of view on her behalf. "I figure since I knew my mother for more than 30 years, I could do my best to reflect on how this story affected my life and how I viewed her."

I would regularly tell this story to my friends after they met her for the first time. I did this because I knew the reaction it would get. Everyone would always be so amazed that the polite, happy, laughing person they just met had been capable of this. That is what makes this story so great to hear. Your jaw would drop each time she told it because you would never see it coming from her. She was so much stronger than she ever let on. Those who came to know her well often used the same terminology to characterize her as a "firecracker." She had a drive that was matched by few, but you would never know it unless you saw it firsthand. It always reminds me of the saying, "Speak softly, but carry a big stick." My mom was one of the sweetest, kindest people out there, but don't dare mistake her kindness for weakness. It was something I believe she passed onto me. It was her actions as I grew up that led me to become who I am today, and I am incredibly grateful for it.

The greatest thing of all regarding the brass knuckles discussed in this story is that they still exist to this day. My mother passed so much on to me throughout her years. Her stubbornness. Her kindness. Her grit. But the thing I still cherish owning is the brass knuckles from this story. Much like her mother before, my mother gave them to me when I moved out on my own. I had no idea, despite hearing this story told when I was younger, that she still had them, and I certainly never expected to one day own them myself. Thankfully, I have never had to use the brass knuckles and I have zero intention of doing so. They will remain an amazing keepsake and memory of her since she has passed. I will always hold onto them until maybe one day, I can pass them on to the next generation along with this story.

THE PROVING GROUND

<u>John</u>

Kids are cruel. Sticks and stones may break my bones, but words can never hurt me. Wrong. That shit actually really hurts. I spent most of my childhood being bullied or picked on. I was the awkward kid that transferred from a private to a public school. It went about as well as anyone would expect. It didn't help that I was about five foot two inches and around 90 pounds soaking wet either. I was picked on ruthlessly for the longest time. To this day, I still remember one kid in particular named Eric.

I had worn a uniform my entire life in private school and learning to wear the types of casual clothes meant for public school wasn't something me or my Mom knew much about. I had decided on a pair of what most would call high waters, which were on the verge of becoming capri pants. Not a smart choice for the first day of public school and Eric picked up on this quickly, asking me where the flood was, making sure he pointed out to everyone that the new kid was lame and unstylish.

I compensated by asking my Mom after that dreadful first day to immediately take me to the store and we bought the biggest, baggiest pair of pants I could find. I showed up proudly the next day, feeling confident in my new stylish jeans and I was ready to show that I could be one of the cool kids too. During recess, I walked past Eric looking to make a better impression this time. I heard him say, "Dude, nice pants. Much better than yesterday." I looked over at him, taking it as a genuine compliment. The new pants worked like a charm. I was going to be a cool kid.

"Wanna be friends?" he asked.

I was secretly elated, although I maintained a poker face acting like this was something I should expect to happen and not make a big deal out of.

"Sure," I replied.

"Well, that sucks because no one likes you. Also, your pants look dumb. Nice try idiot."

Ouch. That one stung a little bit. Some of his friends were nearby and began to laugh at me, adding insult to injury. I wasn't going to be a cool kid after all.

I continued to be the nerdy weird kid for quite some time. I eventually made plenty of friends and figured things out as most kids do. Interestingly enough, Eric would become one of my friends later in life and he doesn't recall ever saying this to me, but then again, we all do dumb things as kids.

It's stuff like this, paired with the constant teasing that I endured that lowered my confidence for a long time. I also never really stopped getting picked on. It was just more low-key than before. I stayed physically small for a long time and I never stood up for myself. I knew that had to change. I just wasn't sure how.

My first attempt at creating change was to start lifting with a friend of mine during high school. I calculated that if I became big and strong, people would somehow respect me for it. Over the course of a year, I actually became pretty ripped but still managed to somehow look skinny. I just had that kind of frame. It didn't change my coolness status either because, despite all the physical gains, I was still emotionally compromised. All the muscle in the world couldn't change my lack of confidence, and it definitely didn't stop people from continuing to bully me. It was unfortunately just the status quo at this point in my life.

However, there was one day where I took a giant chance. A leap of faith that would change me in more ways than I could ever imagine. I decided I wanted to train in martial arts. It was so far outside of anything I had ever done before, but something needed to change. I normally wasn't much of a risk taker, and this was going to push the limits of my comfort zone, to say the least. I secretly called a gym in a nearby town and begged my Mom to take me, which she reluctantly agreed to do. From the very first punch I threw on the very first day, I became obsessed. Each day I got to train, I would look forward to opening the door and being greeted by rock music playing loudly, the sounds of a punching bag being knocked around, the humid air, and the smell of sweat and hard work. I trained as often as I possibly could. It woke something up inside of me that I never knew was there. If I could have chosen to, I would have lived in the gym.

I was training primarily in Muay Thai Kickboxing and Brazilian Jiu Jitsu. These were the sports that would become very popular since they are featured heavily in the UFC (Ultimate Fighting Championship). In fact, it wasn't long after I joined that the sport exploded in popularity, which was fine by me. More popularity meant more training partners, which meant more challenges. I was not a natural by any means, which meant that I had to work hard to keep up with my peers. I was smaller than everyone too, which meant I got smashed, but I didn't care. Every time I got beat, which was frequently, I would get back up and try again.

Training in martial arts just became something I did. As the years passed, I graduated High School, moved out, and got a job, but I lived for the gym and nothing else. Admittedly, my personal life suffered a bit. I ruined a relationship, my work suffered and what little college education I was attempting to get was suffering as well. All I wanted to do was go to the gym. It was part of my routine, a form of escape from the day, much like someone likes to wake up with coffee in the morning before starting the rigors of the day, I woke up looking forward to kicking someone in the head.

I never really discussed my training with friends or family. They all knew I did it, but truly had no idea how obsessed I had become. I would occasionally visit home with a black eye, and everyone would joke that I was getting beat up again. They encouraged me to stop and told me I should focus on my career instead. They thought a small guy like me didn't really have a place doing this kind of stuff. Man, this pissed me off. My whole life I had been the skinny little kid who was told by those same friends and family that I needed to put a little meat on my bones or stand up for myself. Now, here I was, taking action, getting stronger, feeling more confident and the only ones knocking me down now was them.

In the end, their negativity just pushed me harder and I started competing in jiu-jitsu tournaments constantly. Looking back now, it was an unhealthy amount of competition. I think I kind of understood it then too but chose to ignore it. At one point I even stopped telling my coaches how often I was competing. I didn't want the added pressure. I wanted to prove myself. I remember one year I competed at least 20 times, sometimes driving hundreds of miles to a tournament, and I probably only had coaches with me for 3 or 4 of those.

I kept everything on the down-low while I kept chipping away, trying to improve myself each time I stepped up to compete. I started winning about 75% of the tournaments I was entering, and I rarely missed the podium. While everyone else had teams and friends and family there to coach and cheer them on, I never invited anyone. Not my parents. Not my friends. No one. They had no idea.

Perhaps that is why they reacted the way they did when I gave them the big news. It was time for me to take another step forward and to test myself further. I was going to compete in mixed martial arts. I was going to fight.

I'm not sure I had ever seen my parents look more horrified. I genuinely believe they thought I had been indoctrinated into some sort of Fight Club cult because their innocent little helpless child would never do such a thing. My friends didn't get it either. They thought my weird hobby had just gotten a bit out of control and most people tried to talk me out of it. They had no idea why I would want to do such a thing, but I was desperate to prove to them and more importantly, myself, that I wasn't all the things they told me I was. I wasn't just some skinny kid who was the butt-end of all the jokes. They couldn't comprehend why I had such a chip on my shoulder. They had no idea what the years of verbal and physical abuse had done to me. They weren't there to see me cry myself to sleep from all of the bullying. They weren't there when I was fighting off depression; starting to believe all the terrible things people said. They weren't there when I thought maybe everyone would just be better off without me around. They just weren't there.

It was different now. I was different. I wanted to show them who I was and what I was capable of, not just to prove everyone wrong, but to introduce them to the new and improved me that they didn't know existed.

I worked with my coaches and a local promotor to set a date, about 6 months out. I also secretly worked with a different promotor to sign up for a pankration fight, which I would use as a warmup. Pankration is basically the same as MMA, without any strikes allowed to the head. In other words, you can hit only to the body and all submissions are still legal. It's a lower-risk fighting style meant to ease people into the real thing. I had never been in a real fight before, so rather than go straight into the real thing right off the bat, I thought this was a good idea to start with.

The pankration match took place on my 23rd birthday. The only people there to see me were my coaches and some of my teammates fighting on the same night. No friends. No family. No cheering section.

I absolutely dominated my opponent. Within the first few seconds, I threw a hard leg kick that made him grimace. I think he got the sense that I had him outmatched on the feet, so he began working to take me down. After I threw another clean combination, almost making him fall to a knee after yet another hard leg kick, he rushed in, pinning me against the cage. He managed to lower his level before I could defend and swept my legs out from under me, putting me to my back. Little did he know, I'm actually a better ground fighter than I am a kickboxer. He dug his own grave. I quickly swept him to his back and wrapped my legs around his head and one of his arms. I connected and squeezed my legs to cut off the blood supply to his brain. You have 2 choices when this happens, either tap and give up or take an involuntary nap. He chose the former at one minute and thirty-four seconds of the first round. I felt ready.

After that fight, the other fighter and corner actually complained to the promotor that I was sandbagging. They said there is no way that I was an amateur with 0 fights on my record. I must have been a liar. I took it as quite the compliment and it actually gave me just the boost of confidence I needed. There was no looking back now.

A few days later, I got together with my coaches and set a training schedule to prepare for the real thing. I stuck to a very regimented diet that would help me lose weight in a safe manner. I walked around at 155 lbs., but my contracted fight weight was 145 lbs., which meant I had some work to do. I made it my mission to be the first on the mats and the last one off every night I trained. I sought out the best men and women in the gym to teach me everything they knew. I was not going to lose. It was time to show everyone what I was made of. I invited everyone I could think of. Friends, family, and everything in between. I was putting myself out there in a way I never had before.

My training went perfectly. Oftentimes, fighters are plagued by injuries during training, but I did everything right. I was in tip-top shape and before I knew it, I was at the venue, only one day away from the fight, completing my weigh-in. I had spent most of my day in a sweat suit, cutting the last little bit of water weight remaining and I managed to make my weight without any major struggles. Now, it was time to rehydrate, eat some good food, and get mentally prepared for the following day. As I stepped off my scale, I looked across the room towards another fighter standing on another scale that had been set up. He wasn't very tall, maybe 5'8" with short brown buzz-cut hair, but he was built like an absolute tank. He was shredded from head to toe, but what stood out the most were his arms. They were insanely big, very disproportionate, and almost unrealistic compared to the rest of his body. He stood there on the scale waiting for the official to call out his weight as he wore a mean look on his face the entire time. "I would hate to be his opponent," I thought to myself.

"One fifty-nine!" I heard the official say. Ugh. That sucks. I knew what this meant for him. He was probably supposed to make 155 and didn't quite get there. He was going to have to go for a run in a sweat suit to cut the rest of the weight when he was most likely already exhausted. I watched him look down in disappointment as he stepped off the scale and I started on my way out the door, my mouth watering, trying to decide what I was going to eat first.

"Hey! Hang on a second" someone called to me before I could get out the door. I turned and saw the promotor running over to me, waving a clipboard trying to get my attention.

"What's up?" I asked him. He looked at me, taking a deep breath. I could tell his news wasn't good. I glanced quickly back to the fighter hopping off the scale.

"That's your opponent. It seems he isn't going to make weight."

"No shit," I replied sarcastically. "The official said one fifty-nine, right? How did he miss that badly? That's fourteen pounds. What the fuck?"

"I know, I know. I'm not happy about it either," the promotor said putting his hands up indicating for me not to kill the messenger. He could tell I was pissed. "Do you want me to cancel the fight? It is well within your rights and I think everyone would understand."

I didn't hesitate. "Not a chance. I didn't invite all these people for nothing."

Out of the corner of my eye, I saw my opponent walking towards me. I turned to him as he approached and stared straight through him; eyes like daggers. Surprisingly, once he reached me, he stuck his hand out, looking to shake mine.

"Sorry bout' that. I overheard. Thanks for accepting the fight still."

This mother fucker. I looked at him for a moment. There I was, looking like God damn Skeletor from cutting to a weight I had never been at before and he didn't look diminished in any way. He wasn't sweaty or pale like most people are after a weigh-in. He looked completely normal. As far as I'm concerned, this was intentional. I don't believe he even tried to cut weight. He hedged his bets hoping that I would accept the fight regardless, automatically giving him a huge advantage. I was livid.

"No problem," I said, finally reaching out to shake his hand for a moment. He began to walk away and just before he went through the door I said, "Good luck" in a cocky, arrogant tone. I wanted to convey that I had caught on to his little plan and I was going to make him regret it. He hesitated for a moment, looked back at me with just a quick glimpse, and walked through the door.

Fight day was finally here, and it couldn't have dragged on any slower. I got to the venue and wandered around during some of the preliminary matches, talking to the people who showed up to watch me. They kept asking if I was actually going to do it, which was typical and frustrating. Here we are at the fight, where they showed up to watch me and they still have doubts that I will go through with it. Why did they consider me to be such a coward? I clearly needed better friends. I just wanted to hear my name called over the speakers so that I could do my little walk-out and get in there. I wasn't nervous to fight. I was nervous to wait for the fight to happen.

As time continued to crawl, my fight was slowly inching closer. I went back to the locker area to get my hands wrapped and begin my warmups. I was ready. As I sat there, eating a last-minute banana, mentally preparing myself, I would occasionally hear the roar of the crowd in the arena reacting to something happening with the current fight. Depending on the type of crowd reaction, you could tell whether it was just a good shot landed or some type of fight-ending action taking place. It was actually making my anxiety surface a little bit, so I decided to drown out the rest of my time before the fight with music.

Just as the song Wars by HURT began playing in my ear, the fight coordinator popped her head through the door.

"You're up next!" I looked to my coaches who nodded their heads at me. I gave them the thumbs up and went to the staging area, where soon my name would be called, beckoning me to the cage where I could finally prove to everyone what I was capable of.

The staging area is a dark hallway with a carpet pattern reminiscent of an old hotel that hasn't been updated since the '70s. The only light that made it in was the bright white lights that illuminated the cage in the center of the arena, shining through the rectangular glass slits in some of the doors leading out there. The air in there was humid and musty from the sweat of other fighters as they gathered around, watching their teammates make their walk to the cage. While I waited, jumping up and down, keeping my body warm and loose, I kept reminding myself why I was doing this. Every single bully that ever picked on me. Every person who refused to believe in me and still didn't. Every time I didn't believe in myself. It was time to show them they were wrong about me. It was time to prove my own inner thoughts wrong. I could do this and I had every right to believe I could. I could do it regardless of what others think. I am so much more than what they think of me.

"And nooowwwww. Making his way to the ring, Joh......" I allowed the announcer's voice to fade away as he called my name. It was my time. The slow rumble and thumping of my walk-out music began to play as I stepped through the doors and into the arena, making my way to the cage. Suddenly, the sound of the crowd, nearly 1,000 people, began to roar as I made my way.

When you step into the cage, especially at the amateur level, they don't give you much time to breathe or acclimate. There are typically a lot of matches for these types of events and they push through them as quickly as they can giving the audience the most bang for their buck. I walked up the 3 or so steps and stepped through the door into the cage as they immediately shut it behind me. The mats felt cold under my feet as they had a slight give to them with each of my steps while I walked towards my corner. I kneeled down and spoke to my coaches who were on the other side of the fence below me.

"You've got this!" they shouted to me. I nodded my head, stood up, and turned to face my opponent.

The referee was already standing in the middle ready to kick things off, looking towards me to confirm I was ready to begin. My bulky opponent was across from me, hopping up and down, wearing the same intense look on his face that he had at weigh-ins. I stared back at him, trying to look through his soul. The music cut. The sounds of the crowd came rushing back in again. People were shouting my name, cheering for me. At the same time, I could hear people shouting his name, rooting against me. My heart began to pound. Adrenaline coursed through my veins as I leaned forward ready to attack. The ref raised his hand above his head, looking side to side as both my opponent and I gave him the thumbs up and then suddenly dropped it hard to his hip.

"FIGHT!"

It was on.

I immediately took control of the center of the cage. My opponent was bigger than me, so I had to control the distance and space in front of me. I was taller and lankier than him, so it was my goal to keep him at the end of my punches and out of his range. I made the decision before the fight that I wanted to get any delusions out of this guy's head that this was going to be easy for him. I wasn't going to let him bully me with his size advantage. After gauging each other's movements for a few seconds, I timed him resetting his feet as I threw a double jab, backing him up on his heels. While he was off-balance, I followed up with a hard head kick. He got his giant arms up just in time to block the kick, but the grunt he made when it connected indicated it did the trick. He shot in to try and take me down. As he dropped to his knees while rushing forward and trying to wrap his arms around my legs, I managed to keep my hips away from him while shooting my legs backward, breaking his grip, allowing me to land with all of my weight over his back. I kept the back of his head buried in my chest while I made him continue to carry all my weight as he did his best to keep driving me backward. Eventually, I felt my feet touch the cage, which acted as a fulcrum for him to keep pushing me up until my back was now against the cage too. I was actually very well versed in fighting with my back on the cage. I had drilled this a thousand times. However, with him being so much bigger than me, staying in this position was too high of a risk. He could lean on me and try to wear me down. I couldn't afford to stay here long.

As he continued putting pressure into my chest with his shoulder and oversized arms, I fought to hook my left arm under his right armpit and reached to the top of his head with my right hand, cupping the back of his head. I used the underhook to lift him up while using the other hand to snap him down and back towards the cage. I side-stepped him at the same time allowing me to spin him around and reverse our positions. Now he was pinned against the cage. I immediately started throwing knee after knee, one of which got up into his ribs. I felt good. After landing a few more knees, I felt him really begin to fight and struggle, so rather than burn myself out trying to keep him there, I pushed myself back out of his range and went back to my plan of keeping him at a distance.

I worked diligently for the rest of the round, peppering him with punches and kicks. He had a bloody nose and parts of his face were starting to swell. I was as fresh as could be.

In any fight when about 10 seconds are left in the round, someone working for the event is given the task of loudly smacking two pieces of wood together. This loud, very unique sound gives the fighters and the corners a heads up that the round is about to end. Many fighters who are down on points will rush in trying to do something significant after hearing this sound to try and leave a good impression on the judges, which is exactly what my opponent did. As we heard the 10 seconds left sound he suddenly rushed in, pushing the pace. I attempted throwing a push kick to keep him at distance and not allow him to get in too close, but he saw it coming. He side-stepped my kick, causing me to miss and before my foot could come back down allowing me to reset and defend, he threw what could only be described as a leaping left hook, catching me squarely in the temple and I crumpled to the ground like a sack of potatoes.

All I could hear was a loud ringing as I stared up at the bright white lights trying to figure out what the hell just happened. I scrambled on the ground like a fish out of water, thankfully protecting my face out of instinct as he stood above me trying to finish the job. I managed to push off the ground and get back to my feet, but my legs felt like Jell-O. I was a sitting duck. My breathing became more erratic and labored as my mouth hung wide open. I remember thinking about how badly my entire face hurt as my opponent was in front of me trying to take my head off. I felt like I had been hit by a lead pipe. The horn sounded to end the round, giving me a much more personal connection to the saying *saved by the bell,* as I stumbled back to my corner, clearly in a lot of trouble.

The break in between rounds was a confusing blur of chaos. It was nothing short of a miracle that I actually made it to my corner without falling flat on my face. There was a zero percent chance I could have told anyone how many fingers they were holding up. I occasionally would shake my head up and down, pretending like I could actually understand what my coaches were saying when really I was trying to figure out which of the two versions I was seeing in front of me was real and which was the result of the double vision I was experiencing.

"Seconds Out!" the referee called, indicating there were only a few seconds left in the break. This meant the coaches needed to leave and the fighters should get off the stools to be ready for the action to continue when the horn sounds again.

The second round began, and I moved back out, trying again to take control of the center of the cage. I was acting out of well-rehearsed instinct that had been beat into me during the last months of training. For some unknown reason, my opponent never really smelled the blood that was clearly in the water. I expected him to rush in and try to take advantage of my clearly still very wobbly state. Instead, he seemed rather content for most of the round to land the occasional punch or two, never really having much of an impact. As time ticked by, I slowly started to get my legs under me again and my coordination began to return. That's when I got a little too ahead of myself and threw a leg kick, causing me to lose my balance and nearly fall backward. I could hear his corner screaming at him to run in and finish it. As he followed orders, rushing in full speed ahead, I saw an opportunity that would make him regret this decision. I planted my feet, bent my knees ever so slightly, and launched myself forward into the air for a flying knee that slammed into his jaw, snapping his head back and causing his knees to buckle temporarily from the impact. He wouldn't be doing that again anytime soon.

The crowd was all on their feet, going crazy and screaming at the top of their lungs, acknowledging that we were putting on a hell of a fight. Unfortunately, for the remainder of the second round, I was on the receiving end more than I wanted to be. With each punch, kick, or takedown that he landed, I could hear the crowd react. I was just trying to survive at this point and recover enough to mount a counterattack in the 3rd and final round. I finally heard the clapping sound signifying there were only 10 seconds left. This time around, I was the one that began pushing the pace. I rushed in, getting right in my opponent's face landing a few punches before placing my hands to his chest and aggressively pushing him towards the cage. He bounced off the fence, putting additional momentum towards me as I threw a kick to his ribs that made him fold over in pain.

"Got him!" I thought to myself.

I moved in, looking to finish him with the few seconds that were left, but he turned back towards me, catching me off guard as he fought through the pain in his ribs and launched a left hook from the hip with all of his might. Even though I saw it coming, there was little I could do. I wasn't going to be able to get my hands up in time, so instead, I quickly planted both my feet and leaned back at the hip, trying to evade the punch and watch it fly past me. It wasn't good enough. Although he missed the majority of my face, he still managed to catch only my nose from the side. He didn't touch a single other part of my face, so all of his force was released as he basically ripped my nose from the rest of my face.

The pain was immediate. It was a blinding, piercing pain I had never felt before. I knew with certainty he shattered it and if I had any doubts, the fact that it opened up like a faucet, streaming blood from both nostrils, was a good indicator. If I didn't know better, I would have assumed my nose was sitting on someone's table in the audience. The horn sounded, saving me again. I looked up at my opponent through squinted eyes, still clenching my jaw through the pain of my nose, and saw he was more or less hobbling his way to his corner too, nursing the rib that I had just kicked. It didn't look good from him, but it looked far worse for me as I turned to walk towards my corner holding my insanely crooked nose, leaving a voluminous trail of blood on my way there.

"My nose is super broken," I said calmly to my corner as they rushed towards me, placing the stool on the ground for me to sit.

"Can you continue? Do we need to stop the fight?" my head coach asked.

"Not a chance" I replied. I watched as they both nodded with a slight smile showing they approved of my decision.

"You need to get back to doing what you did the first round. He's starting to look tired and he's hurt. Fuck it, you're both hurt, but you're better than him. Keep your distance and keep him at the end of your punches. Make him miss and make him pay. Got it?"

I took a last sip of water and stood up, looking them right in the eyes. I could hear the crowd still screaming loudly in the background. I knew there were people out there watching me, rooting for me. I am either going to win this thing or go down swinging. I handed the water back to my corner and said, "Let's do this."

My corner left as I turned to face my opponent. I opened my mouth, taking as deep a breath as I could with a nose that no longer functioned properly. I looked straight at him and smiled smugly to let him know I was coming for him. The only thing missing from this moment was the song Eye of the Tiger slowly getting louder in the background as I prepared for the final five minutes of battle. The horn sounded and the third round began. I immediately went back to taking control. I felt reinvigorated. I adapted my plan a bit to stop him from rushing in and catching me again with those hooks anymore by throwing inside leg kicks to chop his legs out from under him each time he tried to move forward. After I connected and he reset his feet, I would pepper him with a few punches, always keeping him moving backward. I never wanted to let him feel like he was comfortable. If he was always moving his feet trying to get set, he couldn't counter, and that was the only way he had been catching me. As the round continued, I kept feeling stronger and stronger. I began changing the cadence of my punches, so he couldn't time me for counters even if his feet did get set.

My plan was working perfectly. He had no answer, and his frustration was becoming clear. He got sloppier and sloppier in his attacks and each time he missed I would fire back, connecting with my own punches. This was my round, and he was running out of time. He began to get desperate, shooting in for another takedown that I quickly stopped. As he pushed backward from the poor takedown attempt, I threw a straight right punch down the middle, smashing it into his nose, flattening it against his face. It was an eye for an eye, or in this case, a nose for a nose.

I could sense how tired he was getting. Unlike him, I had trained my ass off for this. While he and his stupid weight advantage were trying to take the easy route, I was working harder than ever. I wasn't going to have it. I wanted him to regret ever stepping in the cage with me.

For the final time that night, we heard the wood smack together. 10 seconds to go. There would be no rushing in this time though. I had thoroughly beat him this round and rushing in the last round left me with a broken nose. I learned my lesson. He was clearly too exhausted to rush in anymore, so I kept my distance while throwing combinations, making him cover up, doing nothing more than defend and survive.

The final horn sounded, and the fight was over. I put one hand up to signal my victory as I turned to walk towards my corner. Suddenly came a loud thud as everything went dark for a second and my head rattled back and forth from some sort of impact. I felt another set of hands on me, pushing me away while I tried to figure out what just happened. I was having difficulty opening my eyes since my face was once again consumed with blinding pain. I turned and saw the referee standing between us yelling at my opponent, pointing for him to return to his corner, while he held his hands up to his chest, palms facing outward acting like he did nothing wrong.

Good Lord did my face hurt. I was holding my hand to my eye trying to put pressure where the pain was coming from. I pulled my hand away looking at my palm, which was now covered in fresh blood. Damnit. First my nose and now my eye.

"I didn't hear the horn! I'm sorry!" my opponent yelled defending himself from the referee's verbal assault.

The audience was booing loudly. Everyone knew this was a late shot and there was no way he didn't hear the horn. Just a cheater from start to finish. Through all the booing I heard my corner yelling to me, "Get your hands up! Show em' you won!" I immediately rose to my feet and shot my hands to the sky. The crowd changed from boos to cheers. I could feel the rumble of their voices. It energized me even more.

The ref came over and told me how awesome our fight was, giving me a pat of approval on the shoulder. I walked towards the center of the cage, still nursing my eye that would barely open. I could feel the skin tightening as it continued to swell further. My opponent and I stood next to each other with the referee in between as he grabbed my right hand and my opponent's left. I watched as the announcer entered the cage, scorecard from the judges in hand, ready to announce the victor.

I ran back through the fight in my head while I waited for the decision to be announced. I was certain I had won. The first round was dominated by me. He knocked me down with 10 seconds remaining, but I had beat him badly for the other 4 minutes and 50 seconds. The second round was in his favor, no doubt about that. The third round in my opinion should have been scored as a 10-8 round. He didn't do a single thing noteworthy other than a late punch. This fight was mine.

"Everyone put your hands together for these two amazing competitors. What a fight!" said the announcer, his voice booming over the speakers in the arena. "And now, your winner by split decision....... Kev........."

I fell to my knees as the sound of the announcer faded. I could no longer hear the audience, the rumble of their cheers, their hands clapping together in support. How could this happen? I lost?......... I lost.

I got up to my feet, turned around slowly, and walked out the cage door that had now been opened for us to leave. The pain all over my entire body was temporarily gone as I walked through the door in a state of confused disbelief, only barely making out the sound of muffled boos of disapproval from the crowd. It seems they didn't agree with the judges either.

I made my way back to the fighters' locker room area and sat down in a chair, while my team surrounded me, telling me I did a great job and that I got robbed by the judges. I didn't care. All I knew was that I lost. There were no words anyone could say to make this feel like a win when it wasn't my name being called through the speakers.

A doctor came in to see me, as was standard procedure. He looked me over and let me know I should go to the ER. I had a broken nose as suspected, which I would need to get set. He managed to address the giant gash under my eye from the late punch by gluing it shut.

"Good job out there," he said as he got up to walk away reiterating that I needed to go to the hospital for my nose as soon as possible.

"Thanks, I guess. It wasn't good enough though," I responded, still completely dejected.

Typically, after a fight, you go congratulate your opponent and tell them good job or something like that. I wasn't having it though. I never went to congratulate him, and he never came to congratulate me. I think we both had just about enough of one another. I wasn't trying to be a sore loser, but between his missing weight and a late punch, I was none too keen on being cordial with him anymore.

Instead, I sat there filled with a sense of dread because next came the difficult part. Before heading to the hospital, I had to go out into the audience and talk to some of the people that came to see me. I slowly walked back down the hallway. The same musty hallway that I went through only minutes ago, fresh as could be, nose much straighter, and eye less swollen. I went through the doors, almost squinting as the bright lights above the arena caused my now pounding head, to pound even harder.

I was almost immediately greeted by cheering. I looked up at the cage to see what the excitement was about, but the next fight hadn't started yet. The cheering was for me. All of my friends and family had congregated around the fighter's area, waiting for me to come back out. I never expected this. I thought it would just be more jokes about me getting my butt kicked, but instead, they patted me on the back, shook my hand, and hugged me.

They told me I got robbed and that I did great. For the first time since falling to my knees in defeat, I actually mustered a smile with my severely swollen face and probably would have cried if both of my eyes were functioning properly. I did it. I had finally proven myself. Not just for them, but for me. I had laid every bit on the line to show them I was more than they or I ever imagined. I won that night. I don't care what any judge has to say about it.

Reflection

For anyone who has ever competed in MMA, it probably isn't that big of a deal to them. For some people, it is pretty intense and for others, it might not be that much pressure at all. For me, it was so far outside of my comfort zone. I had so much internal pressure built up towards this, that it felt like it meant everything at that moment. I don't mean to overstate anything or to claim that I am good enough to be some kind of world champion. In fact, that is not the point here. The point is, I wasn't the things I had been told I was my whole life. I was making my own path in my own way. This fight was symbolic and would help define a major part of my character going forward through my entire life.

I look back on this now and wish I could tell myself that I had nothing to prove. What did it matter what these people, who weren't very good friends anyway, thought about me? I don't regret the fight or competing at all. In fact, I went on to compete many more times and still actively train to this very day. However, I wish I would have just done it for me. As individuals, we place too much value on what others think of us. It is easier said than done but going through this really helped me get over that slump in my life. I continue to train and compete because I like it. I encourage others to do it as much as I can too. It has provided me both good friends, mentors, and a confidence that has permeated every aspect of my life. These are all things that can be accomplished without the validation of others.

I don't believe I will ever stop training because doing so pushes me. I'm proud of what I do. Now, each time I watch someone walk through those gym doors for the first time with a chip on their shoulder, I immediately gravitate towards them. I see my former self in them, and I know their struggle. I make it my mission to be their guide and help them succeed in seeing that they too are so much more.

The Ugly

THE LINEUP

Betty

The son of a bitch was drinking again, but this time was much worse than any of us had ever seen.

Even my mother seemed more worried than she normally gets. At the time, I was 11 years old, making me the oldest of the children, all girls, and the youngest of us was still just a baby. It was the Great Depression and life got harder with each passing day. Money was tighter and more difficult to come by. Struggling was part of everyday life.

Life as we knew it left many people drowning their sorrows in alcohol. I wish I could attribute the same reasons to my father's habit. My father had been an alcoholic my entire life. We had no idea what caused him to turn to the bottle though. Everyone understood that he had lived a difficult life, but there was never one incident that someone could point to, including him, that led him down this path. It was just the way he was.

Thankfully, he was a very handy guy so he found work wherever possible. It was one of his only redeemable qualities, but it wasn't enough to keep the mouths of nine children and his wife full. This burden and his self-perceived failure to provide for his family took an immense toll on him.

He was a complete and total failure as a father in my opinion, but not as a provider. We knew what hunger was, but I certainly couldn't say we were starving. We knew what pinching pennies was like too, but we still had clothes on our backs. There were many families worse off than us. If there is one thing I could find to respect in the man, it was his work ethic. It was his only legacy I'm glad he passed on to his daughters. He can keep the rest to himself.

When prohibition ended, it further enabled his alcoholism, and as our living conditions worsened through the depression, so did his drinking. He would often come home already 3 sheets to the wind and the clear jug; oh that fucking jug; that he continually reused, would almost be empty. I hated that stupid jug almost as much as I hated him. I would see it sitting around the house in random spots, sometimes full, sometimes empty, and I would weigh the risk versus the reward of breaking it right then and there. If it stopped him from drinking for even one night, I thought the beating I was sure to receive might be worth it, but I never worked up the courage to follow through with it.

Like most people, when my father drank he went through a range of emotions. However, his were usually just varying levels of anger. The more he drank, the more his rage would surface. I had lost track of how many nights all nine of us children huddled in the single room where we slept, trying to comfort one another as we listened to our mother on the receiving end of his alcoholic outbursts. We all knew just to stay out of his way, but sometimes you were just in the wrong place at the wrong time. Everyone had felt his anger at some point. It was a vicious and seemingly endless cycle of drinking and abuse. Our mother was running out of excuses to tell our teachers when we showed up to school with bruises and black eyes. It was probably even harder to explain her own. I think the teachers knew what was going on but didn't dare speak up. Times were tough, and we were not the only children facing this kind of dilemma. We were nothing special.

But that night his drinking felt different. My father paced throughout the house, sweat pouring down his head. He seemed anxious, distracted, and lost in thought, only stopping occasionally to take yet another pull from that god damned jug. He was doing his best to hide whatever was going on with him, but it was clear something was wrong. Very wrong. He was completely unhinged. His rage was palpable, making the air feel heavy. There was no doubt that something bad was about to happen, it was just a matter of how bad it would get.

As a few of us completed our chores for the night, keeping a careful, watchful eye on him, he suddenly stopped and took a long deep breath while slowly closing his eyes. Once he opened them and looked up, he slowly turned his head, taking a moment to look at each one of us. He examined us in the way you would look at a wall. There was a sense of disconnect, like we were nothing more than objects passing by in front of him, unimportant and insignificant. After a few more moments passed, he finally spoke up.

"It's time we all had a talk." His voice sounded somber and sad in the same way someone might tell you there's been an accident. "All of you go downstairs. I'll be down in a minute."

He looked at my mother for a long while and she stared back, fearing what he would do next. I could tell that his demeanor concerned her as he stood there, waiting for us to follow his directions. I remember he had the eyes of a completely defeated shell of a man, glazed over and lifeless; no compassion; no kindness left. He was nothing more than a cold, callous stranger to us.

We all gathered into the basement and huddled around my mother, who was holding her youngest, trying to keep her from crying. I was doing my best to stay calm and prepare for what was about to come. What could we have possibly done to deserve this? What did we do wrong? How bad was he going to beat us this time? My palms were sweating profusely as my heart raced and my breathing quickened. Tears were welling up behind my eyes. I felt trapped and helpless like the walls were closing in around me.

The sound of the slow, methodical thumps of my father's footsteps as he made his way down the stairs snapped me out of it. I looked to my mother. She handed the baby off to one of my sisters. Then she stood up, pressed her hands to her mouth, and stared towards the stairs with a look of sheer terror on her face. I looked back at my father and immediately my heart shot into my throat as my body became consumed by fear. There he was, standing at the bottom of the steps, double-barrel shotgun in hand with the break open perched over his forearm. He was coldly staring at each of us.

"Ed?" My mother spoke softly, clearly trying to maintain composure and keep everything calm.

"What are you doing, Ed? Put the gun down and let's talk about this." I watched as a single tear began to run down her face.

"There is nothing to talk about, Mary." My father responded, his voice resolute and unwavering.

My mother's voice became more hurried and desperate. "Ed, please. No. Don't do this. Please."

"We're done talking, Mary............. Let's make this quick."

He turned to all of us. "Stand up against the wall" he calmly ordered, as he held a single finger pointing to where he wanted us to go. No one moved. We were frozen; scared and confused as he just stood there, waiting, while a few of my sisters began to quietly sob. My entire body felt heavy, crippled by fear. I just wanted to curl into a ball and cry. *Am I going to die?*

"NOW!" he shouted.

His scream made me jump and shutter. I looked to the ground and began to move to the wall with my sisters. As we lined up, side by side, my mother suddenly rushed to him and began desperately clinging to him, beating her hands on his chest, crying, pleading for him to stop. He reached up and grabbed her by the hair, yanking her head backward, before he pulled her head back in close to his face.

"Mary!" he growled her name, jaw still clenched shut. He was losing what little patience he had.

"Mary!" she began to struggle against him.

"Ed. Please no. No. No. No." My mother continued to cry and plead with him.

"That's enough!" he said as he pulled her head back and threw her to the ground.

I tried to be strong, watching my mother struggle against him. She was on her knees, shaking as she violently wept. I kept fighting off my tears as she got back up and stood in front of him again, her hands clasped and interlocked, held against her chest.

"Ed………….." She couldn't fight back her emotion and getting any words out was proving to be difficult. But he just stood there, staring back at her, never even so much as blinking.

"Please, don't do this," She begged him one more time.

"Go with the children, Mary," he said calmly, looking at our mother with tears streaming down her face.

She slowly turned and walked back to us. She stood in front of us, her back to our father, and dropped to her knees as we all huddled around her. She had done so well to shield us from the monster our father had become. But this time, there was nowhere to hide us. Our father had enough of his life. In his mind, I'm sure he had justified what he was about to do. He couldn't keep us fed while he was alive, and we were certain to starve with him dead. I think he thought he was sparing us from further suffering, fully believing this was the only way.

There was no escape for us. Nowhere to run. No will to fight. Just the four white concrete walls of our basement that had become our prison, closing in around us as my father began slowly walking towards us. My body shook, as he closed the break on the shotgun, making a loud snapping sound. I was trembling with fear, but deep down, I began to feel something burning at my very core. I was angry. I was so angry. How dare he! How could he!? What kind of person does this to his children? I no longer wanted to cry. I wanted to kill him.

I looked away from the others, huddled together, trying to comfort one another as the end neared. I turned towards my father, took a single step towards him, and decided to look him right in his cold, dead eyes as he approached.

My gaze caught his attention. I expected him to say something to me. This was supposed to be the part where his 11-year-old daughter stands up to him and snaps him out of it, or maybe he would comment that my sudden bravery was misplaced and that he could see how scared I truly was. I didn't honestly care what he said, I just wanted him to say something and face me and stop being a coward.

Instead, he said nothing. He just stared at me as he raised the gun, pressed it against my forehead, and pulled the trigger. My eyes closed and my body tensed, awaiting the impact. My mother let out a horrible shrill scream. Then it went quiet, and all I could hear was the sound of my heart beating so loud I thought it was going to burst from my chest.

Click.........Click.........Click. Click. Click.

Nothing. I was still alive.

I opened my eyes to see my father still standing in front of me with a confused look on his face. He pulled the gun away and opened the break. He looked down the back of the barrel and let out a disappointed sigh as he mumbled something to himself. He had forgotten to load the gun. The alcohol had gotten the better of him.

A few long moments passed before he finally spoke.

"This isn't over, so don't even think about leaving. You have nowhere to go."

It was clear he was speaking to my mother as he looked back at her before turning to walk away. This was the time to run, right? I looked to my mother, seeking reassurance that we were on the same page, but the look of complete and utter defeat in her eyes confirmed that we were not going anywhere. We would do as he said because everyone already knew what happened when you disobeyed, and this time was no different. I had made my valiant last stand, but it seemed our fate was sealed.

My father slowly walked back up the stairs. After he disappeared, I fell to my knees and began sobbing uncontrollably. I looked again at my mother. She was doing her best to keep the kids calm and make everything feel like it was going to be okay when she knew damn well it wasn't. I watched her as she looked at each of her children, carefully examining the details on their faces, taking everything in, assuming this was the last time she would see them. As she did this, I noticed the look on her face change. She stopped crying and her focus seemed to shift. The look of defeat was gone. Now it was replaced by determination and resolve, something I never really saw in her before. She rose to her feet, slowly, steadily, with purpose, took a deep breath and without missing a beat, not a word spoken, walked forward, and marched up the stairs. She wasn't going down without a fight.

Now, it was just me and my sisters, alone and scared for our lives. I went over to the other girls. As the oldest, it was my responsibility to comfort them while we waited for something, anything, to happen. But this was too much. I couldn't shake the sense of impending doom that was hovering over us. We were going to die. He pulled the fucking trigger! What are we supposed to do now? I wanted him to come back down and just get it over with. I wished the gun would have been loaded so that this suffering could just end.

At the top of the steps is the door leading outside. If we sprint for it, maybe we could make it. No. He would hear us. Where would we go after that anyway? My mind raced to think of a way out of this hell, but there was nothing. This was madness. I felt like I was going insane, watching the clock slowly tick as the seconds went by, which turned into minutes, which turned into an hour. We waited for a struggle to ensue upstairs, but there was nothing. As each little noise occurred here and there, even a simple creaking of the walls, it would send a jolt of terror down my spine. The silence in between was almost too much to bear. I wanted to pull my hair out. I wanted to scream. I wanted to go grab the gun and do the job myself. Anything to free me from this nightmare.

My head jerked back towards the stairs. Footsteps. This was it. Here he comes. What do I do? He is going to kill us.

Just then, our mother peeked her head through the doorway as she continued quietly down the steps. She had an immense look of relief on her face as she whispered to us that everything was alright. We were going to be okay. I almost fainted. I was preparing myself for death and now everything was going to be, okay? How? What did she do?

We followed my mother as she led us up the stairs, occasionally reminding us all to be quiet and to go get ready for bed. As we cautiously made our way to our room, we passed near the living room, and there he was. When I saw him, I stopped in my tracks. My heart began to race again, and my throat dropped into my stomach. I immediately sank back into a pit of despair. What was she thinking, bringing us right back in front of him? I took a long look at him, waiting for him to say something, but he was just sitting there in his chair next to the lone dimly lit lamp in an otherwise dark room. The shotgun was perched against his leg with bullets strewn across the end table next to him, most of which had fallen to the floor. It took me a moment to notice his eyes were closed. He was more slouched in the chair rather than sitting up. His chest was slowly rising and falling with each breath he took. From the looks of it, he must have passed out while attempting to load the gun. This was the image of a broken man who had given up. You don't get any lower. This was the bottom.

The thought occurred to me that I should sneak over there and grab the gun myself. Then I could be the one who showed no mercy, no remorse, as I pulled the trigger. I took a single step forward towards him but much like that stupid jug, I couldn't work up the courage to go through with it.

I felt a hand rest on my shoulder. I turned to look back up at my mother who was now standing next to me. All the other children had gone into our room. She looked down at me, shaking her head side to side as she placed her index finger to her lips, telling me to keep quiet and then pointing for me to follow along and go to our room.

I didn't sleep that night. How could anyone sleep after something like this? I worried about my mother, wondering if she would be okay. I was just lying there in a cold sweat, waiting for him to walk back through the door and finish what he started. I stared at the door, afraid to even blink, waiting for it to open so I could watch the silhouette of my own father kill each of his children in their sleep.

However, these images in my head never came to pass. As the night went on, it gave way to the morning, I watched the sunlight slowly creep through the single window in our bedroom. Everyone was awake and although it took a while, we finally mustered up the collective courage to step out of our room and see what awaited us.

As we stepped out, much to our surprise, we were greeted with the sweet aroma of ham and the sounds of kitchen utensils clinging and clanging together as our mother finished making breakfast. I took the lead, walking further out towards the kitchen. The sounds grew louder as I turned the corner towards the table, where our father was sitting behind his newspaper, reading, like it was any other normal day. As we all gathered around the table, unsure of how we should behave, I briefly glanced over to the living room. The shotgun was gone and so were the bullets. Bullets that only hours before, were meant for us.

My Mother peeked her head out from the kitchen. I could see a quick break in her overly friendly demeanor, startled and unaware that we had made it out of our bedroom. She quickly put her fake smile back on and announced that breakfast was ready. We sat down and began to eat. No one said a word. The only noises you could hear were the loud chewing of the children, the occasional cooing of the baby, and the clinking of forks or knives hitting the plates. You could cut the tension in the room with a knife. Our mother kept glancing at each of her children, fake smile permanently painted on her face, as our father just sat there only occasionally appearing from behind his newspaper to take a bite of his food.

I thought about taking my knife and stabbing him. He wouldn't see it coming from behind his paper. More empty thoughts with no action though. I couldn't do it, but I had to do something, right? His actions could not go unaccounted for. I needed to be brave and confront him for once in my life. I opened my mouth to speak, but no words would come out. Suddenly, I could feel eyes, like daggers piercing me. I glanced over to my mother and one look was all I needed to understand. I was not going to say a word. We were powerless. We were just going to pretend like everything was okay and that life was back to normal. Back to a time before our own father tried to kill us.

My father never spoke of this day again. No one did. He also never touched a drop of alcohol again in his life. Living day to day with him was like living with a stranger. I didn't know him anymore and I never really cared to try. Although he never admitted to doing anything wrong or acknowledged that this even happened, something did change in him. He went to great lengths to make up for what he had done and tried to become the father he always should have been. He worked harder than ever before to provide for the family, and he even tried to take interest in our lives, but there was no coming back from what he did to us. I never forgave him. None of us did.

My mother miraculously stayed married to him until the very end. She followed not long after he passed. I didn't attend his funeral and I have never visited his grave. He stopped being my father the day he made me stare down the bottom of a barrel. The moment he felt that without him we couldn't survive. The moment he labeled me weak. I would spend my life proving him wrong and prove him wrong I did.

I've experienced so many things that my father tried to take away. I've traveled. I've lived, I've loved, and I've laughed. I have done my best to take in each moment and enjoy every single breath I take. I met the love of my life and have had 4 wonderful children, whom I love with all my heart. They have even had children of their own and I've gotten to experience all the joy of not only being a parent but a Grandparent, too. I've loved my life. Every single moment.

Reflection

Unfortunately, the narrator of this story is no longer with us and the world is a little bit darker for it. In her place, her Grandson has decided to reflect on her behalf from his point of view.

A long time ago my Grandmother shared this story with me. She told me that I was the first and only person she had ever shared this story with. We were incredibly close, and she was one of the most important figures in my life. As I got older, we could always sit and talk for hours about anything. We shared our secrets, and we shared our dreams. She was my greatest teacher and truly helped me become the person I am today.

During one particular visit during the holidays, I was helping her put up decorations, but I could sense something was off. She seemed very distracted and lost in thought. It wasn't like her. I suggested taking a break and as we sat down, I asked her if she was feeling alright. I'm not sure what prompted it, maybe it was the anniversary of when this happened or maybe she was reminiscing about the past. Regardless of circumstance, seemingly out of nowhere, she told me this story.

There is something to be said for her keeping this a secret for so long and why she, nor any of her sisters ever spoke of it. Although she never swore me to secrecy, I kept it to myself as well and never bothered to tell anyone. While she was alive, I felt it was her story to tell, not mine. However, in her passing, I have given this a lot of thought. To know her and not know this about her is a shame. She was so strong, and everyone knew it, but no one other than me knew how strong she truly was. This story was a part of her. A part of her character and the way she lived the rest of her life. The reason why she became the woman we all knew as the rock in our family, stemmed from events like these. My Grandmother went through every day like it was a blessing because she stared death in the face and lived to talk about it. She always made the best of every situation, because unlike most people, she had truly seen how bad it could get. She was truly an amazing person.

I am so happy after knowing this, after learning of such trauma, that she ended up living a long and good life. Sure, it was full of ups and downs like anyone else, but she never stopped sharing with me how good it was to be alive.

THE ACCIDENT

Blake

We hated being away from our parents. Both of us were a couple of Momma's boys. Whenever my parents were away, I could never sleep. The only way I could even get to sleep was my Grandma sitting at my bedside, slowly stroking my hair, soothing me into a deep slumber.

It was Tuesday, October 15th, 1996. I had just turned 9 years old. My 3-year-old brother, Jacob, and I, were staying at my Grandma's house for the week since my mom and dad were on a vacation to see some family.

On this particular night, around dinner time, we all decided to get something to eat. My Aunt and Uncle also lived with my Grandma and all of them were habitual fast-food eaters. They ate out every day, sometimes multiple times a day. It was disgusting.

We decided to go to Arby's since I really wanted the curly fries. My Uncle drove, like he always did, and my Aunt rode in the passenger seat. My Grandma was in the driver side rear seat, Jacob rode in his car seat in the middle, and I took the rear passenger side.

I should mention that Jacob didn't want Arby's, and I'm not really all that sure anyone but me did either. So, I played a childish guilt card. I should get to go to Arby's and get curly fries since Jacob popped my favorite ball only a little while before this.

At my Grandma's house, I would always set up an elaborate pretend bowling alley. I used an inflatable ball and pretend pins with a backstop, which was just a piece of an old school desk that was usually kept in the basement. I was pretty much guaranteed a perfect game every time since the pins didn't really exist and it was up to my imagination to determine how many of them fell. While I was well on my way to yet another perfect game, one of my shots got away from me. While Jacob sat there, minding his own business doodling in his coloring book, the ball cracked him right on the side of his head. I watched his face scrunch up forming all the wrinkles in his nose that he always got when he was angry. His displeasure with the ball was on clear display and he screamed at me at the top of his lungs. I didn't even have time to say sorry before I saw his hand raise above his head, colored pencil firmly clenched and pointing downwards. My Grandma got up, attempting to intervene but it was no use as he swung his hand down sharply, stabbing the ball, immediately popping it with a loud crack. To be fair, the look on his face quickly turned from anger to surprise, to regret as the ball sat there, limp and lifeless. I don't think he thought it would actually pop. I loved that stupid ball, and I used this series of events against him when Jacob said he didn't want Arby's. My favorite ball being popped equaled my choice of a terrible fast-food dinner.

As we drove along, I was giving Jacob the silent treatment and vice versa. We weren't the type of brothers that argued regularly, so this level of disagreement between one another was rare. Thankfully, I sucked at holding grudges. I felt bad making him go somewhere he didn't want to go. I tilted to my left, peering out the front window to see that we were the first car in line sitting in the left turn lane heading onto the service drive where Arby's was located. This was my last chance for redemption. While we were sat at the red light, I finally spoke up.

"You know, we can go somewhere else if no one wants to go to Arby's. It's okay. I promise."

I didn't want Jacob to be sad anymore. For as long as I can remember, I have been terrible at being mean. I don't like the way it makes me feel. It just leaves a bad taste in my mouth and I get stuck ruminating on it all day, if not longer. I often think back to my childhood and wish I could find those people I was mean to and apologize for things they probably don't even remember happening.

The light turned green and we inched forward preparing to turn. In all honesty, I didn't actually think anyone would change their mind, but not speaking up would have made me feel worse than I already did. Offering to go somewhere else was more aimed at relieving myself of guilt than it was a genuine offer. While my body leaned to the side as the car rounded out the turn, Jacob finally blurted out, "No, I want curly fries too!"

I heard what happened next before I felt it. The screeching tires gave way to the sound of Jacob screaming in that high-pitched way only a child can. Horns and the twisting of metal was so loud in my ear it was like I was chewing on aluminum. Glass shattered all around me, glistening as it flew through the air. My head slammed side to side violently like a rough rollercoaster ride. I remember trying to keep my hands towards my chest, but the whiplash sent them flying out of control as we rolled over and over. The world continued to spin, and the twisting metal changed to a snapping and popping sound while the frame of the vehicle that was protecting us gave way. My body and head rang louder with each uncontrollable impact against the door or window next to me as each crack and twist of the car caused the space around me to collapse and cave in even further. It was chaos and confusion as darkness crept in from the corners of my eyes. The world was fading, sounds were quieting, and the edges of reality blurred until I slowly slipped away.

I woke up moments later, or that's how it felt at least. I struggled to get a sense of what was going on. I fought to concentrate and focus my eyes, like staring through a camera lens as it struggles to focus on the objects in front of it. Everything was dark except for the little bits of light from the headlights of other nearby cars peeking through different openings and bouncing off the thousands of little glass pieces strewn everywhere. The smell of burning oil and gasoline filled my nostrils. I could make out car horns still blaring, only barely cutting through the ringing in my head; the first sign of my blown eardrum, resulting in a permanent 90% hearing loss in my left ear.

I slowly gathered myself and tried to take stock of what was happening. Nothing made sense. It was difficult for me to recall where I even was. We were heading to Arby's. The car. We were in a car. But now, I'm stuck, hanging above everyone, being held up by my seatbelt.

That's when the pain hit.

It was so intense and so sharp, and it covered every inch of my entire body. Some areas just felt numb and cold, while other parts felt like someone was holding a lit match next to my skin. I tried to scream but even the effort of that set off a chain of painful jolts from head to toe. It felt like my very bones were being twisted and bent, being pulled from the joints that held them to the point just before they snap. I remember becoming incredibly aware of my breathing. Each inhalation became shallower and more difficult as I began to hyperventilate. I wanted to gasp for air, but the fear of the pain became too much. I was getting light-headed, and it felt like I was drowning. I was so scared. My eyes darted around while I kept my head as still as possible, terrified of what might happen if I moved too much. Panic set in. I just wanted my mom or dad or anyone really to please come and help me.

But, no one came. I tried to cry but I couldn't. I thought I was going to die. I felt hopeless. Then I got mad. I just wanted this to end.

I felt something pressing into my chest. I looked down to investigate. Not far away from my immediate line of sight was my right foot, twisted and facing the wrong direction. My leg was bent at a right angle at about mid-thigh, forcing the rest of my leg below that up into my chest. Meanwhile, the rest of the space that my leg normally occupied between my hip and my foot was basically gone, broken and crushed, forming into an accordion shape.

The world started closing in around me again, but this time I fought it. Everything started to blur as noises occasionally came and went. All of my senses began to heighten as my body began to go cold. My brain began to scream at me, begging me to stop whatever is causing the pain and suffering. But I was helpless, just hanging there, praying that someone would come and save me.

Suddenly, the horn that was so loud finally died, pulling my focus back to my immediate surroundings. The car. That's right. I'm in the car. Where is everyone? I slowly worked up the courage to move my head around, gently and cautiously. I looked to the front of the car. I managed to make out the figures of both my Aunt and Uncle. Their bodies just slouched to the side, limbs hanging lifelessly with no sign of movement. My Uncles body rested against his door with his head sitting directly against the concrete road since the glass was no longer there. I could actually make out the dashed white lines of the pedestrian crosswalk. My Aunt, directly in front of me, was stuck like me, suspended by her seatbelt, one arm hanging across her body while the other came to a rest against my Uncle's shoulder.

What about Jacob? Where is my Grandma?

A voice began to cut through all the ambient noise. It was slightly shaky, quiet, and soft-spoken. I tried to calm myself and lean into the sound since it was difficult to make out where it was coming from.

"My baby, my baby. No, no, my baby. Oh God, no......."

I could hear the distress and despair in the voice. I recognized it, but in my current state of mind, I couldn't quite put my finger on whose voice it was. I started to search for the source voice but moving was still difficult with my leg pinned the way it was. As I jostled around trying to free myself, if only a little bit. I managed to tilt and turn to my left and I was immediately sprayed by some sort of liquid in the face. It seemed the little movement I managed had put me directly in the path of whatever it was. It just kept hitting me over and over in short, powerful spurts. It was getting everywhere, soaking my hair, hitting me in my eyes, and it even went in my mouth. It smelled like metal. It was thick and viscous, and I did my best to spit it back out. I recognized the taste. Like iron. It was blood.

I started pushing my head forward and to the side, ignoring the pain in my leg and attempting to move out of the path of the spray. My body continued resisting, making movement difficult. My breathing began to quicken as dizziness set in from my efforts. I pushed it to the back of my mind and forced just enough movement so that the onslaught of blood was no longer hitting me. I brought my hand up, which was also stained red, and did my best to wipe my eyes, smearing the red liquid all over the rest of my face, desperately searching for the voice cutting through the noise. I squinted and tried to focus through the dark. I finally saw my Grandma. She was pushing her head up against the car seat as her hand slowly stroked Jacob's head and hair.

I hardly recognized him. His face and clothes were covered in fresh blood. I could make out several tiny glistening dots where glass had embedded into his skin. Below his head, there was an odd protrusion at the base of the neck causing the skin to look like it had been stretched and twisted. My nine-year-old brain was frantically trying to comprehend what I was seeing as my Grandma's fingers slowly laced through Jacob's clumped and blood-soaked hair. Just above his right eye was a bulging gash, so deep that I could make out small sections of the white of his skull. This was the source of what was spraying me moments ago as blood pulsed from the wound, timed with each beat of his failing heart. His body spasmed as he choked on the fluids that were slowly filling his lungs. In between spasms, his chest would rise violently, his back arching, while he gasped for air, gargling the blood in the back of his throat with each attempted inhalation. This image is something I will never be able to remove from my mind.

"Oh my God! Oh my God! Someone help! Help, please someone help! Call 9-1-1! Oh my God!"

It was a woman's voice from above me. She sounded panicked. I could feel my heart begin racing again as I tried to take a deep breath and speak up, but the effort shot pain from my ribs deep into my spine. It caused my body to jerk, and I yelped before I quickly reconsidered trying to talk again. The voice began to fade.

Please come back, I thought to myself. Don't leave me. I'm so alone. I'm so scared. Help me, please. Why is this happening?

I felt cold again and reality itself began to shake as I felt myself slowly slipping away. I allowed my eyes to close. I fought as hard as I could but could no longer resist the pull into the darkness. The chaos began to diminish. It was calm here. The muddled sounds of suffering faded. It was quiet here. So, I let go and sank ever further away from the light.

I woke to the high-pitched sirens of fire engines winding down after their arrival on the scene. I fought

hard to remember where I was as I peered into the dark
car from the back seat watching the blue and red lights
flash every few moments onto the features of the interior.
I couldn't shake this sickening feeling that something was
terribly wrong. I glanced up, looking into the night sky. A
streetlight poked into view. I turned down to my left and
that was all it took to bring everything rushing back. This
time there was no blood spray on my face. No need to
search for a voice I couldn't find. Everything was right in
front of me. My Grandma was still stroking Jacob's hair
slowly, but now she was quiet, shoulders shaking as she
cried, tears streaming down her face before falling to the
seat below her.

If you ever look into someone's eyes and really
focus on them, you can see their life force in some unique
kind of way. Like when you make someone happy, and
you can see a physical light in their eyes shine through. I
pay close attention to this as an adult. I value that light. I
truly believe you can tell a lot about a person by looking
into their eyes. I've often had people tell me my eye
contact can be too intense because of this habit.

My brother's eyes were still open, but that light
was gone. He just stared aimlessly forward, eyes faded
gray and glazed over, looking at nothing. The blood no
longer pulsed from his head, the spasms had ceased, and
his chest no longer rose. I examined him, trying to search
for a sign he was still with me, but there was nothing. I
looked up, making eye contact with my Grandma and she
stared back at me. Her breathing was slow and shallow as
her mouth hung open. Her face winced in pain as she
clung to the car seat, keeping herself as close as possible
to Jacob. I wanted her to say something, but nothing
came. Perhaps she was searching for the words to say or

perhaps she knew there was nothing that could have possibly been said. So, we just stared at each other in silence, crying and plummeting further into our own new hell. There was no light left. He was gone.

Our silent eye contact was abruptly broken as I heard someone say, "We are going to get you out of here, okay?" The voice got further away. "It's real bad, John."

Another Firefighter approached, stood next to my window, and began asking questions to gather info on the scene. My Grandma, being the only one capable of speaking intelligibly, began answering the few questions asked by the first responders. A few moments later, amidst my absolute confusion and stupor, a blanket was placed over my head. Then came the deafening noise of twisting, scraping metal only inches from my head. It felt like the accident was happening all over again.

The Firefighters cut the door off my side since it couldn't be opened normally. The next thing I knew, there were gloved hands, that smelled strongly like a bonfire around my head, holding me gently on each side of my face. That touch meant everything to me. I might as well have been in that car for days; cold, alone, scared, and unsure if I was going to be alive after my eyes closed again. That touch gave me something to feel and something to hold on to. Something to drown out the noise and fear. I just focused on that touch, letting everything else, all my surroundings, all the noise, just fade away.

I eventually came to, unaware of just how much time had passed. As I opened my eyes, I could see the shine of bright white florescent lighting above me, and I could hear the beeps, timed with my own heartbeat to my side. The pain was immediate. All too often, whether it be after a hard workout or after a hard fall, people use the expression that they feel like they had just been in a car wreck. Let me be the first to tell you that you have no idea what that actually feels like. My nervous system couldn't even keep up as I clenched my teeth, feeling sharp pain like needles piercing every bit of my skin. If I didn't know better, I would have told you that someone was actively sawing through my right leg with a dull blade. And the headache, oh my God. I remember literally thinking that if I could just pull my head off, maybe then I could get relief.

I felt a hand touch my arm. The pain wouldn't allow me to turn my head, but I managed to look to the corner of my eyes to see my mom sitting next to me. Her mouth was moving, but I couldn't make out the words. Her face was withered and tired-looking. Her normal cheerful demeanor had been washed away by grief. Mascara was running down her cheeks, following the path laid out by the tears streaming from her eyes. As she put her head down, resting her forehead against my arm, I looked to the end of my bed as another figure came into view. My dad was standing there in the corner, quietly crying, his hand moving side to side as he pressed it lightly to his forehead. I may not have been able to hear the words he spoke next, but it was easy enough to make them out from the movement of his lips.

"I'm so sorry. I'm so, so sorry."

The devastation they were going through is immeasurable. As they sat next to their oldest child, watching me struggle to breathe, struggle to move, struggle to stay alive in an ICU bed with tubes coming out of me every which way, they were also reeling from the loss of their youngest. Although seeing me alive was probably some sense of relief, the reality set in that they would never see my brother alive again. They wouldn't see that little crooked smile of his anymore. They wouldn't wait with him at the bus stop on his first day of school or feel true terror as he learned to drive. They wouldn't see him experience all the joy and pain of being alive ever again. He was gone.

The beeping of the monitors quickened next to me. My mom lifted her head back up, a look of concern spread across her face as her mouth began moving, speaking to someone in the room that I couldn't see. The pain had begun to overwhelm me and the trauma of what occurred began to flood back in. Images of my brother's bloodied face and twisted neck came rushing back. I could hear the crunching metal, screeching tires, and my brother's scream all over again. It felt like a weight was being set on my chest. I wanted to cry but couldn't. The effort was too much.

"Here we go. This will help."

I could finally make out a voice. I didn't recognize it.

"Shhhhhhhh....... We're right here. We're right here, baby." My mother's voice finally cut through the fog of flashbacks and pain.

I darted my eyes back and forth around the room as everything began to feel fuzzy and warm. I spotted a calendar on the wall. Friday, October 18th. How long had I been unconscious? I squinted harder and harder as the calendar slowly went out of focus. My body began to feel like it was floating as the walls around me began to melt into waterfalls. I spotted a clock on the wall near where my dad was standing. It had about 20 different symbols, none of which I recognized, floating around in circles as the minute and second hands spun around past them at a hundred miles an hour. The voices continued in the background but became slow, deep, and muffled, like I was listening to Charlie Brown's teacher. The warmth in my body melted the pain away. My eyes felt heavy. Time to sleep.

The police and fire crews that were on the scene explained everything that happened to my parents based on witness testimony and investigations afterward. As our car turned at the green light, another car blew the red light at around 40 mph, hitting us in the passenger side rear door, right where I was sitting. The car that hit us careened off into the ditch while our car pivoted on the front tires before rolling three times, eventually coming to a stop on its side against a minivan sitting at the opposite light. The driver of the other vehicle, a woman in her early 20's, was drunk and on a myriad of other substances they would later find in her system. Even worse is that the passenger, her boyfriend, was completely sober, but police assumed that since his license was suspended, he had her drive despite knowing her condition.

The road to recovery for everyone was like walking through a field full of landmines. We knew going into it there would be trouble and most likely, not everyone would make it. My Uncle managed to walk away with only a concussion and some lacerations. They kept him overnight for observation before clearing him the following day. He never recovered mentally though. He blamed himself, even though he did nothing wrong. He stopped taking care of himself over time, allowing his body to deteriorate from alcohol and poor life choices. A few years later, the demons he had fought off for so long got the better of him and he took his own life at the end of a rope.

My Aunt broke her neck and suffered several significant blows to the head upon impact. It permanently paralyzed her from the waist down, confining her to a wheelchair, and has wreaked havoc on her memory and cognition skills. Not long after my Uncle passed, she had forgotten he ever existed.

My Grandma had 2 crushed vertebrae, a shattered wrist, and 3 broken ribs. She had to have multiple surgeries on her wrist and would spend nearly 8 weeks in the hospital before finally being released. She was never the same again. She had dealt with trauma in her life before, but nothing can prepare you for something of this magnitude. The rest of her life was spent caring for my aunt while taking as many pills as the doctor could prescribe to numb both the physical and emotional pain.

As for me, I had a broken femur, 8 broken ribs, 2 shattered vertebrae in my neck, a broken ankle, a broken wrist, a broken orbital bone, and bruised lungs. I went through 5 reconstructive surgeries on my leg and one more for my wrist while spending 21 weeks in the hospital, relearning how to walk. In the meantime, life just passed me by as the world kept on turning. I never got to attend my brother's funeral. I barely made it through 3rd grade, or any grade after for that matter. I didn't witness the struggle of my parents going home after visiting me each night, trying to cope with everything that happened. I wouldn't watch them drift apart. I wouldn't see the night my dad didn't come home. When the hospital released me, it was just me and my mom in the house. She tried so hard to be strong, but her pain was too much. She turned to the bottle as a coping mechanism and slowly faded away, becoming nothing more than a shell of her former self. My dad got to visit every Wednesday and every other weekend. I basically just existed in a corner somewhere while he spent all of his time with his new family. He never looked at me the same. I was just a reminder of everything he lost, everything he was trying to leave in the past.

The driver of the other car walked away with minor injuries. However, the passenger, her boyfriend, was killed in the accident. She went on to be sentenced for 1 count of involuntary manslaughter for the boyfriend, 1 count of voluntary manslaughter for my brother, and 4 counts of reckless endangerment along with a DUI to top it off. She served 16 years of her 30-year sentence and was released in 2013, free to live the rest of her life, unlike the people whose lives she took away.

My brother's official cause of death was blunt force trauma and blood loss from a broken neck and severed temporal artery. They told my parents and family he died quickly and most likely didn't feel anything. "Painless," they said. They didn't have to watch him suffer like I did to know otherwise.

This accident and my brother's death became something of a taboo in my family. We didn't discuss it. During one of my mom's drinking episodes that descended into a form of psychosis, she actually went through family albums and systematically tore up or burned all of the photos containing my brother in them. Despite my best attempts to find more, I have only found one photo that she missed during her thorough destruction of her past. When she later passed away, they forgot to even put my brother's name in the obituary. No one ever confronted the past. They just tried to hide it, burying it deep, so far away that it was like he never existed.

It took me 14 years to discuss the accident with anyone. My Grandma was in failing health. It smelled like crappy hospital food as I sat next to her bedside in the dimly lit nursing home room, while we were having one of our many long talks about nothing in particular. My mind was beginning to fail me. For quite some time, I had been descending into a dark hole that I didn't see a way out of. Each time I closed my eyes, all I could see was my brother, dead and covered in blood. I couldn't sleep. Eating didn't interest me any longer and suicidal thoughts were becoming a routine part of my day. I could be standing at a crosswalk waiting for the light to change and I would start contemplating what it would be like to step out into traffic. I tried therapy and pills along with everything else under the sun, but nothing helped.

My Grandma was one of the few people in the world that I trusted with anything. During a break in our conversation, I finally decided to reveal my secret to her. That I remembered it all. The noise. The crying. The pain. The death. Every bit of it. Most of all, I remembered her. I wanted her to know that she had not been alone and that she will never be alone in remembering what happened. She took a moment to think as she wiped away a single tear that formed in her eye.

"It has been so hard to sleep, hasn't it?" she said. It was an odd response, but one I understood. All the times that I would stay over at her house through the years, she would hear me thrashing from the nightmares. I have relived this accident a thousand times in my sleep. I remember her waking me from these nightmares and telling me it's going to be okay while running her hands through my hair until I fell back asleep, just like she did for my brother in his last moments.

I sat there crying, confessing everything to her as she lay there. I dropped to my knees, knelt at her bed, and buried my head into the sheets sobbing uncontrollably. As I tried desperately to compose myself, I felt her run her fingers through my hair once again, to help comfort me one last time. She knew what I was going through because she was going through it too. She was stronger than I would ever be. She was experiencing all the same emotions, yet there she was, comforting me like she always did. She was always able to wake me from my nightmares because she had already woken from her own. We knew each other's suffering and I will forever live with the regret that it took me 14 years to tell her that I remembered it all.

This was one of the last conversations I ever had with my Grandma. As her body gave way, so did her mind, and after a few more weeks her health took a sharp turn for the worse and she passed away in her sleep. At least she could finally get some rest.

My life will never be the same. All I can do is move forward and make the best of what I have been given. There is no happy ending to be had here. There are just people trying to find a way to cope with the pain and carry on in his name.

Reflection

Where do I even begin with explaining something like this? It's a story that I don't enjoy telling, so I don't tell it, typically to anyone, but here I am finally letting it out. Not a day goes by where I don't think about the accident. Not a day goes by where I don't miss my brother. I'm admittedly in more pain than I will probably ever let on. I don't cry, not because I'm heartless or soulless, but because if I cry, it all comes back, and I can't stop. I don't like doctors or pills, not because I don't want help, but because it reminds me of 21 weeks spent with doctors shoving pills down my throat to help me "get better".

I made the choice to finally tell this story for two reasons.

First, I hope telling this can be something therapeutic for me, and maybe, just maybe, I can start moving past it. I have suffered from some form of PTSD for most of my life after this. To this day, the sounds are what cause me to have anxiety or panic attacks. I hear them in the back of my head, playing on repeat, and they don't go away. I can be having a normal conversation with people and while my mind wanders these noises blast through, silencing the conversation around me. I don't bother telling people why I seem off, because then I always have to see their same sad face feeling sorry for me. Maybe one day I can process this properly. I have finally been making the effort to do so, and I believe telling this story here for this book is a step in the right direction.

The second reason is drunk driving awareness. I didn't hold back on all the gruesome details because I want you, the reader, to understand what this event has done. The scariest part of this story is there are so many others just like it, or even worse than mine. Every time someone who has read this gets behind the wheel of a vehicle drunk, I want them to remember this story. They need to realize that they could be the next cause of events like this in someone else's life. Ask yourself, is it worth it? Life is precious. Please protect it and be responsible for your actions. Go out and have fun. Just have a DD or use an Uber to get home. That's all I ask.

I doubt the pain will ever go away. I look around at what little family remains or keeps in touch when the holidays come around, wondering how different it could be. Everyone feels like a stranger to me. These events caused so much trauma for so many connected to it. For now, I try to live my life and put one foot in front of the other. I will live on for him and do my best to be happy. I love you and I miss you, Jacob.

ONE UGLY GARGOYLE

John

Being on a fire department isn't all it's cracked up to be sometimes. Don't get me wrong, it's definitely one of the most rewarding professions out there. You get to go and help people every single day while working with some of the best people on earth. However, there are some not-so-fun moments too, like waking up at 2am on a shift for a routine call while you are only half awake. It's part of the job, but no matter how much you love doing something, doing it at 2am when you were just in a deep sleep only moments ago can be a bit trying for anyone.

It was the middle of winter in the Midwest during an especially bad cold snap. It was the kind of cold where the local weather channel tells you not to go outside for more than 10 minutes or risk frostbite. On top of that, there had recently been multiple nights of snow in a row. Depending on where you were located in town, some areas had really bad snowdrifts.

At around 1 a.m., when it was at its coldest as temperatures dipped well into negative territory, the fire tones went off, waking all of us from our deep sleep. There was a total of 6 people on shift that night. Four of us were working on the engine and two of us were Paramedics working on the ambulance. It was a pretty straightforward call for an 80-year-old male experiencing shortness of breath. Everyone got dressed and grabbed their gear. We responded to the call with lights on, but no sirens since it was the middle of the night during a weekday and there was very little traffic. No real reason to wake everyone up if it wasn't necessary.

Once we got to the neighborhood where the call was located, the roads were terrible. The snowdrifts in this area were particularly bad for some reason and if I didn't know better, the plows must have forgotten to go through here after the most recent snowfall. It was a much wealthier area with absolutely enormous and immaculate houses, with long winding driveways and columns perching up overlooks above the entryways. Most of them had perfectly manicured bushes and multiple statues in front of the house typically surrounding a circular driveway leading to the massive front doors.

As we arrived at the address given by dispatch, there was a large amount of fresh, deep snow making it nearly impossible for us to clearly identify the driveway. Our Lieutenant made the decision to have both the engine and the ambulance stay out on the road and we would all walk up the driveway with our equipment. That way we wouldn't risk any accidents with the larger trucks. There have been many infamous stories over the years across different departments of arriving to the call, only to get stuck in the ditch and have to call for backup.

The second we stepped out of the vehicles, we were slapped in the face by a freezing cold hand. It stung your nose and cheeks immediately. A strong wind wasn't helping matters much. It caused snow to blow around everywhere, getting in our gear and more importantly in everyone's eyes, obscuring our vision. Each one of us trudged through the ankle-deep snow, dragging our gear along up the never-ending driveway at a hurried pace. Most of us were forced to hold an arm up trying to block our eyes as we headed to the door.

If I had to take my best guess, I would say the house was around 500 yards from the street where our vehicles were parked. During the long jaunt to the door, I tried to take my mind off the cold by looking around and sizing things up. As a firefighter, this is just a good habit to get into, so that you can relay information to other responding units more clearly and accurately if needed.

The moon was shining brightly, giving the many snow-covered bushes and statues an eerie silhouetted contrast to the untouched, reflective snow on the ground. Most of the statues were the more stereotypical types you might picture as you imagine walking up to a wealthy mansion. They invoked religious symbolism and were posed in different more elegant manners. Then, as we approached the home, we came across one particular statue on the lawn close to the door, that you might consider the red-headed stepchild in the family of statues. It was starkly different from the others. It would be better described as a gnarly, haggard gargoyle. It was much shorter, standing maybe only 4 feet tall. It was black, covered mostly in snow, and had more rigid and darker features compared to the others. It just didn't belong. I remembered thinking maybe it held some sort of importance to the owner in a way we couldn't understand and whether or not it fit in with the rest of décor was unimportant to him. Either way, even in the darkness while everyone was focused on the task at hand, we all took notice of this hideous thing.

As our Lieutenant walked past, he chuckled loud enough for everyone to hear over the sound of the wind and said, "Man, that is one ugly gargoyle."

It was exactly what everyone was already thinking. A few of us burst out laughing. It was a nice change of pace, making us forget about the bitter cold numbing the majority of our faces for a moment.

Finally, we got to the door, but something was wrong. The jam on the door was cracked and the wood was broken as the door sat slightly open. There had been forced entry on this door, which indicates this may have been a break-in. We stopped immediately and backed away since this was not part of the plan. We were given no information about this. The call was for routine shortness of breath, which is something we handle every day, but seeing signs of a break-in changes our approach to the call considerably.

Thankfully, as we looked back towards the street while backing up from the door and getting ready to radio in our findings, the police were just pulling up. In our district, it's common practice for police to show up as support on every call when possible, just in case something like this happens. As we saw him get out of his car, we radioed over to him that there was evidence of a break-in and we watched as he quickly picked up the pace, jogging our way while calling for backup.

The officer arrived at the door and asked us to stand back as he announced himself at the top of his lungs while pushing the barely hinged door open the rest of the way.

"POLICE!" he yelled. "IS ANYONE HOME?" He cautiously moved further into the house, gun drawn, as we waited outside. We began to hear more sirens in the distance. Backup was on the way.

We patiently endured the freezing cold outside, unable to see what was happening inside the home. We could only hear the occasional callouts of the officer announcing himself as he entered different rooms, ready for whatever happened next. I was incredibly nervous. I had never been on a call like this before where we discovered a potentially active break-in. The thought also ran through my head that it could be a setup. In fire training, you are taught about people that will sometimes fake 9-1-1 calls to report incidents that don't exist. That way, when first responders show up, they will be waiting in the shadows with firearms or bombs to kill you. It can be a scary world that we live in sometimes.

"Elderly male, conscious, in the kitchen on the floor. This is our call." The officer reported back to us.

It snapped me back to reality. It was nice to confirm that the call was real, at least to some degree. We knew there was still a patient that matched the description of the original call. It was a major relief for me.

It was at that moment our lieutenant decided to call for an additional ambulance just in case there was going to be another person found that we were currently unaware of. The officer inside the building then gave an all-clear for us to come in. He had checked all areas of the home and determined it was safe for us to enter and start treating the patient. Although no additional individuals were found, we kept the additional ambulance coming to be safe.

We quickly got to the patient, who was really struggling to breathe. He was desperately trying to tell us something, but the labored respiration was causing too much difficulty for him to get a single word out. He was frantic. He kept shaking his hands at us and pointing up his index finger as if he was indicating to just give him a second to catch his breath, which wasn't going to happen. It is understandable when this happens since being unable to breathe properly can cause a logical panic response.

The medic went to work as I watched, providing support when needed. We got the elderly man hooked up to supplementary oxygen and an intravenous line was established as well. As medics continue looking over a patient, it's common practice to declare your findings out loud to ensure that everyone is on the same page, creating a more coordinated effort during the chaos that a medical or fire call typically is.

"Several contusions to the neck and head. Lots of bruising on the chest and back. Could be from a fall if he collapsed," called out one medic.

"Understood, let's have someone hold his neck stable, get him in a brace and on the backboard before we load him up," the lead medic responded.

In the back of my mind though, I still couldn't shake the feeling that there was more to this. It isn't impossible to have that many injuries from a fall, but it isn't likely either. The forced entry on the door still concerned me. Hopefully, once we get the patient more calmed down and breathing better, he can help fill in some of the blanks for us.

"DON'T MOVE!!! HANDS WHERE I CAN SEE THEM!" someone shouted as loud as they could just outside the door behind us.

At first, I thought this was the moment where I died. The intruder must have been hiding all along and evaded the officer during his search. Now he had us. I looked at everyone else in the room and they were thinking the same thing. I watched them as most took deep breaths, closing their eyes as they came to terms with what might happen next. We all stopped what we were doing and slowly began putting our hands up. Then more loud shouting erupted with multiple voices all screaming over one another. It was so chaotic it became hard to distinguish what was being yelled, and who was doing the yelling. It was just noise and confusion at this point. The police officer that checked the house, put his hands down and drew his weapon, snapping backward towards the door quickly, ready to pull the trigger if needed. He went to the door where all the yelling was coming from and went outside to investigate. About 5 seconds later he came back and stuck his head through the doorway.

"We need another medic out here."

The rest of us put our hands down and stared at the floor, eyes wide, mouths open, and breathing heavily while coming down from the thought that we were possibly all going to die only moments ago. Once our panic resided and the yelling stopped, the ambulance crew resumed treatment with the elderly man and my lieutenant, who was a paramedic as well, got up to go assist with the officer's request. He then signaled to me to come with him to help with whatever was happening outside.

We walked out the doors and were immediately greeted by the biting cold and wind, which had only gotten worse. Red and blue lights from several police cars were shining everywhere, illuminating the entire scene as the silhouettes of about 5 or 6 officers now stood in the driveway, all huddled around another figure that was sitting on the ground. The figure seemed oddly familiar. Then it hit me.

The gargoyle!!!

I looked over towards the door where the ugly gargoyle was sitting, but it was gone. Now, that very same gargoyle was handcuffed and sitting on her butt, resting against the knees of one of the police officers, mumbling a bunch of nonsense to no one in particular. I quickly did a double-take, thinking this wasn't possible. I shook my head, trying to squint my eyes harder, thinking I was seeing things. I looked over at my lieutenant to see he had the same shocked look on his face that I probably had. He looked back at me, eyebrows raised in a confused manner, and opened his mouth to say something, but nothing came out. We were truly both completely speechless.

We proceeded to approach the girl, formerly known as ugly gargoyle, sitting on the ground and began assessing her condition.

"Hi, ma'am. I'm going to ask you a few questions okay?" I asked, taking the lead while my lieutenant took a step back to radio the ambulance in route that they have another patient. She didn't really respond to me, just scoffed more or less.

"Can you tell me what your name is? Are you hurt or in any pain?" Those questions suddenly got her attention as she made a mocking face at me while moving her lips like she was imitating me asking the questions.

"I'm Serahhh ya duh bitch. None o thos hoes cooowed make hurt enway," she finally said, slurring every word. If it wasn't for my experience dealing with really drunk people from other medical calls, I'm not sure I would have actually been able to make out what she said. I looked up at the cop who had her propped on his leg and asked, "Has she hit her head, or was she injured in some sort of struggle. I just want to make sure she isn't concussed."

He chuckled to himself and said, "Oh no. She's just very intoxicated."

More red and blue lights started shining through the night as the other ambulance pulled up. Two more medics got out and began bringing their cot down the driveway. While they were approaching the home, the group in the house had loaded up the elderly male and made their way out the front door. A neighbor had woken up and walked through the snow over to the driveway wearing nothing but a robe and snow boots. Typical Midwesterner. It's below 0 and they're wearing a robe and boots. This is probably the same person that you'd see out in a short-sleeve shirt and shorts in the middle of winter, claiming the cold doesn't bother them. We may be a hearty bunch, but sometimes not the most intelligent.

"Is everything alright? I…. I… I know the man that lives here, and I just wanted to make sure everything is okay with him."

"Sir, this is an active scene. I appreciate your concern and we will let you know if there is anything you can do, but for now, we recommend going back inside and staying warm," a police officer responded.

While everyone was distracted by the neighbor's arrival and other activity, the drunk gargoyle saw an opportunity. She suddenly lunged forward with all her might, remarkably shooting straight up to her feet. Her effort knocked me backward and my lieutenant quickly moved out of the way putting his hand up towards his chest, palms facing outward indicating he wanted nothing to do with her sudden drunken, yet surprisingly coordinated actions.

She dashed forward, attempting to make a daring escape as everyone looked on. However, it didn't last long. After she lunged up, her intention to sprint away was very evident, but only her legs got the message. Have you ever seen someone standing in a hurricane with gale-force winds blowing straight at them while they keep trying to move forward against the wind despite slowly getting blown backward? It was kind of like that. She fought the wind and lost badly. Her legs began to step forward, but her upper body stayed behind, bending straight backward at the hip and she went down hard, like she had been clothes-lined from an invisible force.

We all calmly walked up to the girl while the police officer quickly picked her up off the ground and propped her up against his knee again. The crew from the newly arrived ambulance had just walked up as well and we placed a blanket around her since she was now covered in snow and was probably freezing. She sat there making a bunch of drunken groans expressing her displeasure with the result of her failed attempt at escape. We began getting her loaded up just as the other crew came outside to take the elderly male to the ambulance.

As he was wheeled past her, he may not have been able to speak his mind, but he did manage to stick both hands out from under his blankets and flip the bird at the woman as she was getting loaded up.

The picture of what happened here was beginning to get a bit clearer now.

Soon afterward, we got the elderly male to the ambulance and began transport to the hospital for him. Eventually, with a bit more difficulty, we managed to get Sarah, the gargoyle, onto the cot, loaded up, and off to the hospital as well. The scene finally began to settle a bit and we took some time to chat with the police officers to figure out what in the hell actually happened.

We spoke with the first backup officer on the scene, the one who shouted hands on your head, making us think we were going to die, and he told it exactly like this.

"I was running up to the home taking a good look and sizing up everything. I didn't see anybody, so I figured you must all be inside already. Just as I was getting close to the door, I couldn't help but notice that ugly ass gargoyle sitting there," he said with laughter. "It just stood out. I walked past it, but then I had to turn and take one more look at it. Something about it bothered me and that's when the damn thing moved!!!" he exclaimed.

Everyone around him began to laugh at the ridiculousness of the situation and that he had the exact same thought as our lieutenant; that is one ugly gargoyle.

"That's when everyone that was arriving behind me also spotted her moving, so everyone started shouting over one another, thinking this might even be a planned attack or something. Thankfully, it was just a drunk girl pretending to be a statue."

Now, allow me to take the time to do some more filling in on the backstory, which we only learned later after everything had been sorted out and cleared up. There is a nice thing about being in the fire service, and that is you get to know everyone in all other services really well. Whether it is the cops that always show up, or the hospital staff that you regularly deliver patients to, knowing everyone really allows you to gather information from all perspectives.

The elderly man with shortness of breath turned out to be just fine, and once he was able to speak again, he told the police and nurses everything. It turns out Sarah was the recent ex-girlfriend of his son, who at the time of the incident was living with the elderly man. She had been out drinking very heavily when she encountered the son with his new girlfriend and became very upset. It turns out the boyfriend still had some of her possessions and she was none too pleased that he had moved on already without giving her stuff back. So, she did the only logical thing that came to her mind and went outside to slash the boyfriend's tires before somehow managing to drive herself to the home of the elderly man.

Once she arrived at the home, she used a crowbar that for some reason she had in her trunk and broke in through the front door. She was immediately confronted by the elderly male who had already heard the commotion she was making trying to get in. After a brief shouting match, they ended up in a fight with one another. Although the homeowner was no spring chicken, Sarah gave up a considerable size advantage, only standing at about 5'2" and probably 100 pounds, but she was fueled by alcohol and rage, which was all she needed to make up for the disadvantage. Unfortunately, during the altercation, the man suffered a cardiac event, resulting in difficulty breathing. Thankfully, drunken gargoyles apparently have a strong, albeit questionable, moral compass, because despite the fact that she just illegally broke into the home, she immediately called 9-1-1, and somehow in her inebriated state managed to coherently explain the situation well enough to the dispatcher, allowing them to send out first responders. However, she then questionably decided that she still had time to go upstairs and get her stuff.

While collecting her belongings, she went on a full-blown rampage, completely destroying the boyfriend's room and lost track of time. That's when she looked out the window and saw our flashing red and blue lights coming down the street. She never heard us coming since we responded with no sirens and by the time she noticed us, it was too late. She booked it downstairs, apparently falling end-over-end down most of them, according to the elderly man who witnessed her trying to get out. She then stumbled out the front door, desperate to escape, but we had already pulled up and were getting out of our vehicles. She had nowhere to go.

That's when she had a plan so absurd, that only the mind of someone as drunk as her could come up with it. She waded drunkenly into the waist-high snowdrift near the door and dove in headfirst. Once she popped back out, she quickly began using her hands to shovel the snow up, onto, and around herself. She then pulled the hood of her dark hoodie over her head and yanked the strings tightly to conceal her face, leaving only the very tip of her nose peeking out. She then assumed a crouching stance and held her arms at her side, bent at the elbows and wrist, similar to in the position of a T-rex's arms.

Lastly and most importantly, she placed every last bit of her remaining drunken focus into not moving. Not an inch.

Her determination to not get caught was immeasurable. Here she was, standing out in the freezing temperatures, wind howling, blowing snow around everywhere, and she never wavered in her decision in the least. In some of the most miserable weather conditions you can ask for, she committed to her actions completely. I love imagining what she got to hear and witness as our fire crew walked up to the door, observing the area and realizing there was a break-in. As we stood there, commenting on how ugly she looked, she stayed crouched, cold, and complacent, manifesting and bringing forth her inner gargoyle, doing everything in her power to not show any sign of life. She didn't flinch. She didn't move a muscle. If this were a movie and playing a gargoyle was her role, I would have tried to start a slow clap in the audience to applaud her performance.

Unfortunately for her, she was doomed from the very moment she enacted this hastily put together plan. Her focus could only last so long given the amount of alcohol running through her veins. She endured not moving while we walked past. She endured being motionless while the police officer did an entire search of the home before calling all clear. She endured so much, but once backup arrived, her focus must have broken, if only for a second and she moved, giving herself away. I oddly admire her effort. She drunkenly summoned more focus than I usually can when I'm stone-cold sober.

Sarah would end up being released from the hospital to spend the rest of her night and possibly some of her near future in jail. The elderly man recovered after a few days and returned home with his son. I do secretly hope they decided to return any belongings of the drunken gargoyle after this incident. If she conjured up this plan on the fly while plastered, I can only imagine how powerful she could become when breaking and entering while sober.

Reflection

I remember reporting back to the station in the fire truck after this call was over. We all sat there, quiet, unsure of how to register just how ridiculous this entire call was. Finally, one of us just spoke up and asked, "What just happened?" and we all burst out into laughter for the rest of the ride back to the station. We kept retelling the story, putting together the pieces from everyone's points of view while laughing until tears ran down our faces.

This story became legendary on the department for quite some time and it is definitely one of the highlights of my career. Honestly, it is best told in person, which allows me the ability to imitate the stance and position of the gargoyle for people. I saw a lot of different things during my years on the department, some good and some bad. However, this one very well might take the cake regarding just weird ridiculous occurrences.

I mean, just think of how insane it is that she nearly got away with it! What a plan! Oscar worthy performance in my opinion.

I wish I could go find her, have a beer with her, and see how much of it she actually remembers. I want to know the thought process she went through to come up with it. It reminds me of something straight out of an old cartoon where one character chases the other until they cut around the corner only to watch the pursuer run right past a row of statues. Then, low and behold, the character being chased managed to imitate a statue before peaking its head out and getting away. Unbelievable.

After this incident, nothing ever surprised me anymore. Once you've witnessed a drunken gargoyle come to life after breaking and entering, I think that means you've peaked. It doesn't get better than that. There was definitely some funny stuff that occurred to me during my career, but nothing was ever crazier or more ridiculous than this was. This was a once in a career or lifetime type of story that I will remember forever.

DON'T YOU TELL ME
WHAT TO DO

Todd

Every year, my company, like so many others, hosts a nice Christmas party for all its employees. Unlike many people though, I actually really enjoy our office Christmas parties. My company goes out of their way to spend a little extra to make sure the employees really enjoy themselves. I also get to work with some of the most brilliant minds in my field of work and this serves as a nice, casual, way to get to know everyone and their families.

There is always really good food served, and a few years prior to this, they started doing an open bar, which has definitely kept things interesting. As one might expect when at an open bar office party, each year there is always that one individual who got too drunk and made a fool of themselves. This year was no exception, but unfortunately, I was way more involved than I would like to be in the "Did you hear about that guy?" story.

My wife Dorothy and I were getting ready to go as we waited for my friend and coworker Jeremy to arrive. I agreed to be the designated driver for the night since I wasn't really much of a drinker to begin with. Originally, I told Jeremy that we would just pick him up, but he had other plans going on all day. So eventually, we agreed that he could park his truck here for the night and the following day we could coordinate getting it back to him.

Our company parties are fairly laid back, but it's still expected that you show up looking somewhat nice. This would be generally classified as business casual. I'm not typically one to dress up or get too fancy. Honestly, I hate it, but Dorothy enjoys the opportunity when such an occasion arises.

"Hey Todd, come here!" she yelled across the house to me. I was impatiently waiting, ready to go, just sporting a nicer button-down shirt and a pair of dress slacks as I got up off the couch and walked back into the bedroom. Good thing Jeremy was late too, otherwise I might have been a bit annoyed.

I turned the corner into the bedroom and stopped immediately in my tracks almost taking a step backward in shock. "What do you think?" she asked. She was rocking some of the most insane knee-high boots I had ever seen. I didn't even know she owned those. Honestly, I thought they were cool, and I wish I would have talked about how great they looked, but instead, I just stood there making slightly unintelligible noises while mesmerized by how crazy they were.

"Actually, never mind. I don't care what you think. I like them and I'm wearing them," Dorothy said confidently before I could gather my thoughts.

I was quickly pulled from my stupor when I heard the doorbell ring. Finally, Jeremy must have arrived. I closed the door to the bedroom and walked over to the front door to answer it. Upon opening, once again, I stopped in my tracks, a bit shocked at what I was seeing.

Much like myself, Jeremy isn't one to dress up. He is a self-described hillbilly from Missouri and proud of it. Also, I just want to be clear that I'm not talking about people who like to pretend they are country boys either. Jeremy literally grew up so far in the boonies that he didn't even have internet access. He often likes to make the joke that he owns two pairs of shoes. First, are a pair of nicer boots. Second, are his "shit-stomping boots" which is what he more commonly wears. And yes, I can confirm they are appropriately named.

He stood in front of me wearing a flannel button-up, with what appeared to be a flannel undershirt of some sort, which made no sense, and a pair of blue jeans. At least it appeared he busted out the nicer boots for this occasion if that is any consolation.

"Hey! What's up? We're late so we should get going," was the first thing out of his mouth.

"I'm well aware that YOU'RE LATE and that we should get going since I've been ready for the last 30 minutes."

"My bad," he replied simply.

"Yeah, no worries. Dorothy is just finishing getting ready so we should be leaving any moment."

"Hey, just so you know, the roads are still pretty icy from the storm so if you want to drive my truck instead of your car, that'd be fine," Jeremy offered. The area we lived in gets pretty cold during the winter and we had recently been getting slammed by winter weather.

Tons of snow, and sometimes it came with layers of freezing rain, adding salt to the wound. I wasn't too keen on driving his truck though. True to form, it wasn't really my style. It was a huge, lifted diesel truck and the thought of Dorothy and her heels getting in and out of it was comical, but not probable.

"No, it's okay. We can just take the car. Thanks for the offer though." This was the first of several decisions I would later come to regret.

Dorothy was ready soon afterward, and off we went. I remember hoping that everyone else brought designated drivers with as well since the roads were worse than I expected. There was still a surprising amount of snow and ice on the ground.

It took a while longer than normal, but after about 30 minutes or so, we arrived at the party. It was about 7pm and the event was scheduled to go until midnight. We walked inside and the venue for this year was awesome. It was a nice local convention center with a big open space made for the nearly 200 people expected to show. There was a dance floor with a DJ and huge, very classy looking bars on each side of the room. We walked over to the front desk and checked our coats. They handed us our tickets and pointed us over to the area where we could pick them up whenever we were ready to leave.

And so, the night began.

After handing our coats off, the first words out of Jeremy's mouth were, "Open bar, dude." We made our way towards the bar and I responsibly got a water like the good DD I was. I turned to the others getting a tip ready in advance for the bartender and asked what they wanted. "Natty Light, please," Jeremy responded.

"Seriously?" I said, questioning his choices.

"Don't shame me, dude. Natty Light, please."

Why in the world at an open bar, where he basically has the entire bar at his disposal, would he choose to go with Natural Light? I shook my head at him while turning over to Dorothy. "How bout' you?" I asked.

"Apple Martini, please," she said with a wide devious smile on her face.

"Oh god! You sure you want to start off with those?" I asked knowing what the consequences of too many appletinis might do to someone.

"Yes. They are delicious and I want one!" Dorothy replied in a jokingly adamant way.

"Your funeral," I said chuckling to myself. Knowing what I know now about how this night was bound to go, I often wonder how quickly she regretted this decision.

The bartender got us our drinks and we went to find a table. However, since Jeremy worked in a different department than I did, he saw a few people he wanted to talk with for a bit and we got pulled into different directions. From this point on, other than the occasional bigfoot-esque sighting, he basically went missing for much of the night.

Dorothy and I moved from table to table or stood at the bar talking with friends, meeting the kids, wives, and husbands they always talk about at work. As I said, I enjoy these things. Now whenever Daryl talks about his wife Suzy, I can put a face and personality to the name. As we continued to move around, we ended up at the bar more times than I could honestly keep track of. I stuck with my choice of water and Dorothy continued with her choice of apple martinis. Oddly enough, I think she was going drink for drink with me, which is a dangerous game to play. My wife is not a seasoned drinker by any stretch of the imagination, and when something tastes as good as an apple martini does, you end up drinking far more than one typically should. I tried to get her to slow down at one point, but it was a lost cause. It had quickly gotten to the point where walking in a straight line would soon become a struggle, so I decided to get her a seat at the bar and grab Jeremy a drink to surprise him with, wherever it was that he went off to.

Turns out though, Bigfoot is very elusive, and I realized now I was the one walking around with a Natural Light in my hand. I thought to myself that I should just toss the damn thing. I don't want to sound overly harsh here, but Natural Light is piss water. The directions on the can should read, open and pour directly down drain.

I turned back around and went to the bar seat where I left Dorothy, but she was nowhere to be found. This is going well. Hopefully, she just went off to the bathroom or something. Next, I decided to just go to the table where I had recently seen Jeremy. Once I made it to the table, walking through a sea of people since the party was now pretty packed, he was no longer there, but thankfully I knew most of these guys.

"Does anyone know where Jeremy went off to?" I asked. I realized everyone was already laughing at something and hardly paying attention to me, so I looked in the direction of their laughter. There was Jeremy, dancing his heart out to what I'm pretty sure was Miley Cyrus' Party in the U.S.A. Even more interesting was that he had a dance partner, and I recognized her. Jeremy worked in the maintenance division and his new companion was the head of maintenance's wife. In other words, he was dancing with his own boss' wife and not in an appropriate *we're just having fun* kind of way. This was going to end poorly, but at least he was having fun, right? I decided it was best to just put the beer down and walk away like I hadn't seen a thing. Time to go find Dorothy.

I didn't make it far before Jeremy suddenly appeared in front of me, already drinking the beer that I had just left on the table. I looked back at the dance floor and then to the table where I left the beer, confirming it was no longer there, trying to verify this wasn't a doppelganger. Nope, he was the real thing. How did he move so fast? Was he some sort of drunken ninja? It was like setting a beer down for him was the equivalent of ringing the dinner bell on the farm for the dogs to come inside for the night.

I tried to refocus my thoughts since he looked upset and was babbling on about something regarding a girl. At first, I thought he must have been talking about his new, albeit poor choice, of dance partners but instead he kept pointing to a specific person standing near another table. I looked over to see a redheaded woman giving Jeremy the meanest look I think I've ever seen someone give another human being. I made eye contact. Big mistake as she quickly flipped us off and walked away from the table.

"She yelled at me! She said she was going to kick me in my piss stain!" he shouted.

I'm not sure why she said this since I quickly looked down confirming that he did not actually have a piss stain to kick. I guess it could have dried already, but that was beside the point. I didn't actually know when this had taken place since it had been nearly 3 hours since

I last saw him. Maybe whenever this occurred, he had recently spilled on himself or maybe he genuinely pissed himself. Regardless of what was or wasn't on Jeremy's pants, he clearly did something to make her angry. This was getting out of hand.

"How much have you had to drink already?" I asked.

"A lot," he responded with that stupid grin of his.

I didn't have time for this. I chose to ignore it and went to go find Dorothy. I was getting a bit worried about her. I figured I would head to the bathrooms first and ask someone going in or out if they had seen her in there. Just then, I caught something unmistakable out of the corner of my eye. It was Dorothy's insane high-heeled boots. I found her! The problem though, is the boots were not on the ground where they should be. Instead, one of them was flying through the air and spiking directly into the chest of one of my coworkers.

My stomach sank to the floor, before lurching back up into my throat. This was not good. I quickly went over and grabbed her arm. "Dorothy! Why did you do that?" I asked.

"I'll do it again if he doesn't stop," she said slurring every word.

This wasn't good. I could lose my job for something like this. Thankfully, one of the guys nearby who was with the person on the receiving end of Dorothy's kick came up to me.

"Don't worry about it. He deserved it. He's being a bit of a drunk idiot and was hitting on her. She told him to stop, and he wouldn't. He deserved it. Hell of a kick, too!" he finished his explanation laughing.

I looked over at the guy getting up off the ground. He looked like he was Jeremy level wasted and I'm not really sure he remembered why he was even on the ground. Serves him right, I guess. Little did he know that my wife has trained in kickboxing and other martial arts for several years, so she is very capable of taking care of herself, even when she is smashed on appletinis apparently. I was honestly fine with what she did, but we decided to just walk away and let it be before things got any further out of hand. I needed to make sure I still had a job come Monday.

I almost considered asking everyone if they wanted to leave early, but despite the open bar and over-consumption, everyone's behavior seemed to even out. Besides Dorothy making the occasional drunk comments about having to kick a guy, she stuck by my side, usually leaning against the closest wall to stabilize herself and pretend she wasn't as drunk as she actually was. Most conversations consisted of me doing some small talk and when I tried to introduce Dorothy, I would have to turn to whatever wall she was leaning against at the time and maybe she would muster a simple, "Hey" while raising her hand up and down quickly before we moved on.

Not counting the few hiccups from earlier, we ended up staying nearly until the very end, having a good time and enjoying everyone's company. However, in the back of my mind, I was genuinely worried about how hammered Jeremy was and Dorothy's choice of apple martinis had truly done a number on her too. I made the decision that it was time to go while they could still make it to my car. The party was winding down anyway, with lots of people getting ready to leave and I didn't want to deal with a long line at the coat check.

If you have ever tried to wrangle a herd of cats before, you can relate to my experience of trying to get Jeremy to leave. He kept disappearing every time I turned around for even a second and generally just did whatever he wanted regardless of my desire to go home. After a little bit of strategic finesse, I finally managed to get everyone to the coat check before the line got too long. Dorothy continued finding the nearest wall to lean on while I dealt with Jeremy's drunken antics, but overall, it was staying under control.

Once we were next in line, I asked Jeremy to give me his ticket. He responded by telling me he was a big boy and could do it himself. I put my head in my hand and acted like I didn't really know him as he stumbled up to the coat check window, which was basically a square hole cut in the drywall, with no additional glass or separator. The woman behind the counter nicely asked for his ticket so she could grab his belongings. Jeremy held out the ticket for her, but as the woman reached for it, he suddenly pulled it back away from her and shouted, "No!" in a childish, playful tone. Apparently, he decided he wasn't done with the party games yet, but he failed to notice that no one else was playing the game but him.

"Excuse me, sir, can I please have your ticket?" she asked again, this time a bit more sternly. She was not amused with him in the least. He held it out once more and as she reached for it, he pulled it back again and said, "No!" this time in a slightly louder version of the same tone. He repeated these actions one or two more times, and it was obvious that the worker was not too happy about his actions. Either she was going to come out and kick his ass or someone from the growing line behind us would do it. I needed to do something.

I walked up to Jeremy and forced the ticket from his hand, telling him to stop screwing around. "What? She's pretty," he said as if that explained his behavior.

I handed the woman both Jeremy's and my ticket. She snatched them quickly to make sure I wasn't playing along with this involuntary game too and went to get our things.

I grabbed the coats and gave Jeremy his things as I turned back and apologized for his behavior. I knew we needed to get out of there quickly before things got any worse. I had Jeremy walk in front of us, making sure he couldn't disappear out of sight anymore. Unfortunately, of all people, the piss stain girl crossed paths with him, and they immediately started bickering at one another again. I still wish I could have figured out what he did to make her so mad and vice versa. They got into it in the same way long-running heated rivals get into it, like an argument between a bitter, divorced couple. Unfortunately, it was escalating very quickly, starting to make a scene, so I jumped between them, grabbed Jeremy by the arm like a toddler, and pulled him along. Dorothy quietly followed and eventually, we managed through some miracle to reach the exit.

A worker kindly grabbed the door and held it open for us. As we passed by, he smiled at each of us and told us to have a good night.

"Don't you tell me what to do!" Jeremy responded without skipping a beat. The guy looked perplexed and as far as I could tell, Jeremy seemed genuinely offended that this guy told him to have a good night. I had never seen him or anyone for that matter, this drunk in my entire life. I again found myself having to apologize for his actions.

"Sorry about that. You have a good night as well." It was the best I could muster given everything that I was juggling at the moment.

Making it to the car was such a relief. Everyone was accounted for and assuming they didn't jump out of the car at some point, we would be good. I locked the doors as soon as they shut just to be safe and started heading home.

As we were driving along, everyone stayed quiet. The silence was music to my ears. I was breathing a sigh of relief that I could get everyone home safely. I needed to do it quickly though since it seemed that Dorothy was doing her best not to pass out and I assumed the same of Jeremy. Thankfully, the roads had cleared up a bit, allowing for a much less precarious and quicker drive home.

I knew there wasn't a snowball's chance in hell that Jeremy would be driving his truck home tonight, so the first stop was his place. As we pulled up to Jeremy's apartment building, I heard a series of very concerning noises coming from the back seat. It wasn't gurgled or strained. It was just a wet sound. The smell quickly followed. Jeremy was throwing up in my backseat.

I was immediately filled with anger. The last thing I wanted to do tonight was clean up puke from my backseat later. I remember feeling immediate regret that I hadn't taken him up on his offer earlier of driving his truck instead.

"Are you serious right now?" I turned around and yelled at him.

"Hey, hey, hey! Don't yell. It's okay, I promise," he responded.

"How is it okay?" I was confused by his response.

"Don't worry guys. I only got it on me!" he said as he raised his hands to show his innocence and success. He wasn't kidding either. The sheer volume of vomit that came out of him was astonishing, but somehow in his drunken state, he had the wherewithal to use his body as a shield and managed to only throw up on himself. I looked around him and didn't see a single bit of it on the seats or floor.

"There is something wrong with you," I said before turning back around and preparing to get out of the car to help him out.

Alcohol is a funny thing, you know. One minute it somehow makes you capable of thinking clearly enough to only puke on yourself and not your friend's nice car, and then the next moment you can throw any semblance of intelligent thought straight out the window. Before I could hardly get out of my door, I heard Jeremy declare, "It's okay. I've got this, guys."

Before I could yell at him to stop, he undid his seatbelt and let it slide across his body. I watched as the strap and buckle scooped up a substantial amount of vomit during their return journeys to the holster. He then opened his door and launched himself out into the cold, spilling any remaining fluids along the side of the car and onto the concrete. Despite his best efforts, he didn't exactly make a soft landing either, as he crashed down face first onto the ground and just laid there making a few groaning sounds.

Now, you would think opening a door would let the smell of the vomit out, but that's where you would be wrong. Somehow, it managed to circulate the smell even more strongly back into the car, where it finally became strong enough for Dorothy, who had been oddly quiet during this series of events, to take notice.

"Oh my God. What is that smell?" she said as she began to wretch. This wasn't good. I had Jeremy, face down on the ground covered in vomit, while Dorothy showed signs of joining his effort. I sprang to action, quickly launched myself out of the car, and ran around to the passenger side, opening the door for Dorothy as fast as I could. If she needed to throw up, that would at least give her the opportunity to do so outside of the vehicle, unlike Jeremy. Next, I ran over to Jeremy and tried to carefully grab him in a spot that wasn't soaked in regurgitated Natural Light. He wasn't being cooperative. If I didn't know better, I would think he had found a nice comfy spot on the cold concrete and was more interested in napping than getting inside. It was like a toddler that you have the carry to rest of the day when they have decided they are done walking and too tired. I've thought a lot about this moment, and I am certain that without my intervention this night, he would have died there. He would have frozen in the cold, lying in a puddle of his own vomit in an apartment parking lot.

After a truly difficult struggle, basically lifting him up while he was dead weight, I started more or less dragging him towards his apartment while he occasionally remembered to move his feet and assist. Before I got too far, I began hearing the same wet sound from before. I almost dropped Jeremy to the ground thinking he was puking again, but I quickly realized it was coming from behind us. I turned, looking over my shoulder to see Dorothy had finally succumbed to the smell of Jeremy's vomit and maybe a few too many appletinis. Thank goodness I got that door open in time and she actually made sure she was keeping it out of the car. After she finished her first round of vomiting, I realized she was going to be fine for a few moments and kept on with my mission to get Jeremy inside.

We didn't make it even a few more steps before I heard, "HEY! HEEEEEEYYYYYY! I'M COOOLLLLDD!"

Dorothy started to yell before round two of the vomiting commenced. This situation was quickly getting out of control and I had no idea what to do. Dorothy was certain to start waking up the neighbors if this kept up, but if I let go of Jeremy, I'm not confident he would have gotten back up again.

I made the decision to push Jeremy as fast as I could to his door. I yelled back to Dorothy, "Hang on. I'll be right there. Just no more yelling, okay?" No response from her came, but it got quiet, so that was good enough for me.

Once at the door, Jeremy got his keys out while using his head as a third arm, by leaning it up against the door for balance, while insisting that he would unlock it. He was so drunk that it wasn't even close. We were never going to get in this way. I ripped the keys from his hand, unlocked the door, and pushed it open, causing him to nearly fall in. Instead, he made it look like he meant to bend over, almost pretending he wasn't drunk anymore. He started trying to take his shoes off while wobbling side to side. Big mistake. It was too much for his drunken brain to handle. Within a moment he went down, face first, spiking his head into a laundry basket so that it flipped back over on top of him. He never managed to get his hands out to help the fall. Instead, his knees bent and hit next, while his ass stayed stuck in the air until he slowly slid forward across his carpet on nothing but his face until he was laid flat out. I always meant to ask him how bad that rug burn must have been on his face the following day, but never got around to it.

I had a good laugh to myself since he kind of deserved it for everything he was putting me through, but I started to feel bad and helped him back up again. I think sliding along his face was a night-ender for him as well since all he could manage to do at this point was repeat through slurred words, "Bathtub. Dude, bathtub."

I wasn't quite sure what he was after, but I followed along and brought him to his bathtub where he quickly stripped down to nothing but a pair of the sweetest long johns you ever did see. At least I figured out what that other flannel-like "shirt" was underneath his flannel button-up earlier. I should have taken a picture for blackmail. Then I witnessed him calmly and carefully lay down and position himself comfortably in his bathtub. He had clearly done this before.

Regardless of how well-rehearsed his bathtub act was, it didn't stop me from worrying if he was safe to leave like this. It was late and I knew it would probably piss him off, but I gave my Dad a call to get his opinion. Once he picked up, I explained my situation. He talked me through everything to reassure me that Jeremy seemed like a seasoned pro and should be fine. "Nobody gets in the bathtub like that as a go-to unless they've been here before," was how he put it. It was settled. Jeremy was sleeping in his bathtub. I put a towel over him, left the light on, and headed out the door back into the cold to go see how my wife was holding up.

As I shut Jeremy's front door behind me, I could hear a car horn periodically honking from the parking lot.

As I looked over to my car, low and behold, I could see Dorothy finishing up yet another round of puking before leaning back into the car and honking the horn several times while screaming, "LET'S GOOOOOOO. I'MMMMM COOOOOLD!"

It seemed my nightmare wasn't over just yet. I figured if she kept this up, it wouldn't be long before the rest of the neighbors woke up, if they hadn't already, and came out to see what was happening. I sprinted to the car, waving my hands yelling for her to stop, which after she saw me, she surprisingly did. I closed her door and avoided stepping the in mixture of Natural Light and appletini on the ground, before getting back into the car and driving off as quickly as possible like a getaway vehicle for a crime that was just committed.

Getting home with Dorothy was much less eventful than Jeremy, thankfully. I got her into bed, where she quickly passed out. I got a glass of water and set it next to her side of the bed, knowing she would want it whenever she awoke from her drunken slumber.

I sat on the couch for a moment and took a few deep breaths, admiring the silence and thanking God that this night was mostly over. I say mostly because, lucky me, I still had one final mission to complete before ending this personal hell that I was stuck in.

I went out into the garage and opened all the doors on the car, letting the smell out. Mission accomplished as I almost began to gag. I opened the garage door next and that finally made the car more approachable, although there was no true escape from the aroma. My senses had been so thoroughly violated at this point that I decided to just go for it. I put on a pair of latex gloves and went to work.

What began as a fun night out at a company party had ended with me in my garage around 3am, cleaning dried vomit out of my seat belt latch. With each scrubbing action, I could vividly recall the wet noise of him puking in the backseat and then him declaring it's all on him. Yeah right. I should've left him in the snow. It wasn't the way I had imagined my night going, to say the least, but at least my misery makes for a pretty fun story for all to enjoy.

Dorothy

FINALLY!!! I get to go out for a night and let loose a bit, even if it is just Todd's company's Christmas Party. I've been looking for a good excuse to wear these new insane boots I got for a while now.

"Hey Todd, come here!" I yelled from the bedroom. I couldn't wait to get his opinion. He came back to the bedroom and his reaction was even better than I hoped for. He just stood there, eyes wide searching for words to say. "What do you think?" I asked, but he just stood there with that dumb look on his face. It would have been nice to hear him say something, but all he managed was a weird mumble. It didn't matter in the end. I knew these boots were awesome and I was going to wear them. "Actually, never mind. I don't care what you think. I like them and I'm wearing them."

Thank god the doorbell rang. Jeremy must have finally arrived and rather than stand there and stare at me like a creep anymore, Todd went to go answer the front door.

I finished getting ready as I overheard Jeremy telling Todd the roads were pretty bad. I think I heard him suggest we take his truck. HA. If he thinks these boots are getting in and out of that stupid lifted truck of his, he's dumber than I thought.

I walked out of the bedroom and into the kitchen to grab and snack. Todd and Jeremy were both standing in the kitchen waiting. Jeremy looked at me and my awesome boots while I looked at him, mildly embarrassed for him that he was going to his work party dressed in a flannel shirt and what looked like long johns underneath. At least it seemed he busted out his nice boots for the occasion.

We got in the car and off we went. I remember thinking I was glad that Todd drove. The roads sucked, but eventually, we arrived safe and sound. We went inside and checked our coats at the front desk. The venue was really nice, and it was pretty cool that it had 2 bars. My boots belonged here.

When we got up to the bar, Todd asked me what I wanted. For the longest time at this point, I had been craving an apple martini. They are just so good. I knew they were dangerous because of how delicious they are, but that wasn't about to stop me.

"Apple Martini, please," I said with a wide devious smile, conveying I knew exactly what kind of trouble I was getting into.

"Oh god! You sure you want to start off with those?" Todd asked. I can't blame him for his surprise. I'm not a seasoned drinker, but that's why we have him as the designated driver.

"Yes. They are delicious and I want one!" I said, completely serious. I'll drink what I damn well want to.

"Your funeral," he said chuckling to himself mostly. I remember thinking he better be careful, or I'll shove these boots right up his ass.

I have no idea where the hell Jeremy went off to after getting what I'm sure was his first of many Natural Lights. Not to be too harsh towards Natural Light or anything, but that stuff is garbage water. If someone ever offered me a drink and then proceeded to buy me a Natural Light, I'm fairly certain it would ruin that friendship.

Todd and I spent the next few hours mingling with other people. It always amazes me how much he enjoys these types of things when most people hate office parties. One of the main talking points at each table, as it should have been, was how awesome my boots were. But Todd is great at small talk. Not me. Once we got done talking about my boots, I couldn't have cared less what little Timmy or whatever their kid's name was, had been up to. So, to avoid any unnecessary conversation I went up to the bar to keep my glass full of appletini as frequently as possible. It was not my wisest of decisions.

I remember Todd trying to get me to slow down, but his attempt to do so came far too late. By that point, I was barely registering where we were anymore. Even walking was getting a bit difficult. The next thing I knew, I was sitting up at the bar by myself. "Where the hell did Todd go?" I remember thinking. But that thought was quickly pushed out of my head because it was time to break the seal.

I got off the barstool and immediately felt like I was walking on a balance beam. The alcohol had destroyed my ability to walk properly, but alcohol-filled bladders wait for no one. So, I managed to make it short distances by going stool to stool and wall to wall, using them to stabilize myself until eventually, the bathroom was within my reach.

I finished up my business in there and knew I needed to find Todd. I continued using my wall hopping technique until I got back into the main party area. I could hear the music for the dance floor being played somewhere near me, which meant I overshot my intended target of the bar. "Shit," I thought to myself. I was really on the struggle bus at this point. The alcohol had gotten on top of me, so I leaned up against the table next to me before realizing there were a couple of guys sitting there just looking at me.

"Hey there!" one of them said as he stood up to get closer to me. I looked at him a bit confused. Perhaps he missed the giant ring on my finger or perhaps he didn't care. Either way, I didn't want to deal with it.

"Sorry, wrong table. My bad," I said as I tried to move away.

"It's okay. If you're lost, I can help you find your way to where you want to be. I don't live far away," the guy said again, dropping one of the stupidest, sleaziest pickup lines I have ever heard.

"You serious, dude? Sit back down before I make you sit back down." I wasn't screwing around. I have zero tolerance for people treating me like an object or for creepy overly aggressive drunk guys. "Ooooo, I like it rough if that's how you want to play," he responded, getting even closer to me.

I think I heard his friends at the table telling him to cool it. Little did they know I didn't need their help and honestly, they should have jumped in more quickly. I have been training in martial arts for years, I've competed in MMA, and I've held my own in the gym against some of the best around. I had warned him I would make him sit back down if he didn't do it himself, so in my humble drunken opinion, the following series of events was his fault.

I launched my knee to my chest, showing off just how awesome these boots truly were, and then launched my foot forward into his gut, just like how you would kick down a door. He immediately went down on his ass and several people turned around to see what the commotion was. His friends at the table all got up to help him while I just stood there thinking, "told you so dumbass."

I felt a hand wrap around my arm. Oh, someone wants another piece, huh? Let's do this. I turned to see it was Todd. Oh, thank God.

"Dorothy! Why did you do that?" he asked.

"I'll do it again if he doesn't stop," was the only response that made sense to me as if Todd would know what I was talking about. Damn appletinis. Thankfully, the guys who were at the table jumped to my defense, admitting their friend deserved it. I think Todd thanked them and we rushed off somewhere to another table.

As I sat down, I remember thinking how nice it was to relax. The remainder of the night gets a bit blurry for quite a while. It comes and goes in flashes. Anything in between is more reminiscent of the 18-minute gap of silence on the Nixon tapes. There may have been something there at some point, but it's gone now.

I can't believe Todd didn't force us to leave after I push kicked his co-worker to the ground, but it seemed like he was having fun again, so I was okay with it. The only thing that truly sucked was moving around again and having to be introduced to people. I mostly would move until Todd came to a stop and then I would actively seek out the nearest wall to lean or stand against. As Todd introduced me, I can only imagine it probably looked like he was introducing his wife, who must have been in trouble for something because she was standing off in a corner leaning against the walls, using her head as a third arm. The only thing missing was my dunce cap. I would usually muster at least a simple, "Hey" when I heard my name said, but that was all they were getting. Stringing intelligent sentences together at this point wasn't happening. That ship had sailed.

The next thing that I can recall is us finally leaving. Jeremy did something to Todd in the coat check line that pissed him off. Then a few moments later, I think the doorman did something to piss off Jeremy. It seemed like everyone was just so mad for no reason. I was just happy we got in the car, out of the cold and I could finally relax.

Not passing out was very difficult during the ride home. I remember losing the battle once or twice, but as my head dropped it hit the window, bringing me back to. We pulled into Jeremy's parking lot first and Todd was mad at him again for something or other and that's when it hit me. It was like being punched in the nose by the smell of someone's insides. It was absolutely brutal.

"Oh my God. What is that smell?" I asked, desperately trying not to wretch, but that battle was lost quickly. I had done such a good job of fighting off any urge to throw up at this point, despite drinking far too much, but this smell did me in. I leaned over and magically the door was open. It's a good thing too because I threw up immediately. I looked around for Todd in between vomiting sessions, but somehow, I had lost him again. It was so confusing. How did I lose him when we were just in the car a few seconds ago? In my drunken state, I couldn't make sense of it and honestly, I was pretty miserable, which was beginning to piss me off. It smelled. I was throwing up. My husband had abandoned me, and worst of all, I was freezing. So, I did the most sensible thing I could think of in my current condition.

I laid on the horn repeatedly while screaming, "HEY! HEEEEEEYYYYYY! I'M COOOLLLLDD!" at the top of my lungs. It worked too, because only seconds later I know I heard Todd's voice say something. So, he wasn't lost after all. I sat back in the seat waiting for him to come back so we could leave and finally go home. I was very over this night.

I closed my eyes for a few minutes probably passing back out, but when I came back to, I was absolutely freezing again. I didn't know if it had been seconds, minutes, or days. Now, I was irrationally mad. I leaned forward to yell something, but then I got another whiff of the smell from earlier. I quickly pivoted and began throwing up yet again. Good thing the door was still open.

In between my rounds of throwing up I was honking the horn again and screaming, "LET'S GOOOOOOO. I'MMMMM COOOOOLD!" I just wanted to go home, and nothing was going to stop me.

The message must have been received because out of nowhere my door was magically shut again and we were peeling out of the parking lot like we had just robbed a bank.

I don't remember getting home after that. All I know is that I was smart enough to put a glass of water next to my side of the bed at some point, and I immediately drank the whole thing. My head was pounding, and my entire body hurt. I lifted off the covers to slowly get out of bed and realized I was still wearing my clothes from last night, including the awesome boots. Todd was already up and about. I made the smart decision to take the boots off, get another glass of water, and spent the rest of the weekend in bed.

Jeremy

Office Christmas parties suck. However, one great thing about our company's party is that a few years before this, they started having an open bar. I have had perfect attendance ever since. Better yet, I had my friend Todd as a designated driver, so this year really had some potential.

I was running late getting over to Todd's house. It took me forever to find where I left my nice boots since I hardly ever wear them. Plus, the roads were complete garbage. I eventually made it over there, only about 30 minutes late, but Dorothy wasn't even ready yet, so it wasn't a big deal. I remember when she came out of their bedroom and into the kitchen wearing some of the most insane boots I had ever seen in my life. Those things could do some damage if you got hit by them. Especially if Dorothy was doing the hitting. I think she trains kickboxing and stuff, so my goal was to not piss her off like usual and I decided not to comment on them. Thinking before I speak has never been my strong suit but having the looming threat of high-heeled boots being shoved up my ass really puts things into perspective.

We took off soon after and I remember being glad Todd drove his car and not my truck like I had offered earlier. The roads sucked and better to crash his car rather than my awesome truck. We eventually got to the party and checked our coats. This place was sweet, plus it had two bars, which meant double the fun for me.

We went up to the bar and Todd asked me what I wanted. I had to make a decision right there. I had the entire bar at my disposal, but at the same time, I was probably going to be drinking for a solid 5 or 6 hours. It came down to a choice of whether I was drinking for quality or quantity. I went with quantity.

"Natty Light, please," I answered. I'm pretty certain he tried to drink shame me, but I didn't care. Plus, Dorothy ordered an apple martini. If she kept that up, she wouldn't last for very long.

I spotted a few of the guys that I work directly with at another table and walked over to talk to them for a few minutes. Once I got over there, they said they were heading up to the bar, but since I had just got a drink, I could hold their seat. Apparently, they don't know me as well as I thought. I chugged down the first beer before they could even get up and went back up to the other bar with them for round 2.

There is a funny thing about alcohol and how it operates. At this point, just before grabbing my second beer, I was very far from drunk. However, because of the sheer number of drinks I went on to have in the next few hours, my memory gets considerably fuzzy starting around this time. It's like a punishment for getting a bit too out of control, as if your mind says, "You know what? You did a bad thing and therefore I'm not going to just erase the memories you had while drunk, but I'm going to take away some of the good stuff too."

The next thing I really remember after that first beer chug is being on the dance floor dancing to something that I was really feeling. None of that Miley

Cyrus type of shit like people listen to now. I don't remember who it was exactly, but I was dancing with someone and I remember everyone at the table daring me to do it, so I went for it. I didn't think it was a big deal, but, for some reason or another, this redheaded woman walked up to me and got incredibly mad at me. She told me she was going to kick me in my piss stain, which is a weird thing to say. I looked down and my pants weren't even wet. Then I finally recognized her as my boss' daughter that he introduced to me earlier. She seemed nice before and now she was pissed. I probably did something that I just don't remember anymore.

Either way, I went back to the table and there was magically another Natty Light sitting there, and everyone said Todd left it for me. I grabbed it and walked away from the table, spotting Todd immediately in the crowd. I talked to him for a little while, but he seemed upset about something or other and walked away.

Everything goes dark for a while again after that until the next thing I knew, we were standing in the coat check line. There was a really pretty girl behind the counter that I was having a friendly conversation with, but then Todd got mad at me again for no reason and made us leave really quickly. Then, of all people to run into again, we saw piss-stain girl who berated me, yet again for God knows what, and thankfully Todd stepped in to split us up because I'm pretty sure she was going to hurt me. Then we were going out the door and some snooty doorman said something stupid to me, so I yelled at him. Not sure what he said anymore, but he deserved it. Leaving that place was such a hassle.

Everything just went a bit dark after that. Next thing I knew, I woke up in my bathtub in my long johns with a towel over me to keep me warm. Been here before. Whenever I know I might be going hard in the paint for a night, I always wear long johns under my clothes in case I throw up on myself. That way I can strip down and sleep in the bathtub for the night in case I throw up again. It's a solid tactic I have employed many a time. I figured since I was already in the tub, I should just turn on the shower. Once I was out, I grabbed another Natty Light out of the fridge and went on with my day. Lawn wasn't gonna mow itself.

Reflection

Todd

Although Jeremy might disagree, this story has been fun to tell our friends and family many times over. He does not remember this night as fondly as others because it doesn't paint him in the best light, but oh well. He still laughs about it when he can.

The unique thing about this story pertaining to me is, I never really drank or attended parties growing up. All of this was very new to me. In fact, at this point in my life, I had never been really drunk before. A buzz, maybe, but hammered, never. I was completely ignorant about how to handle this situation. At the time, I was seriously worried about the condition Jeremy had put himself in. However, through the years of being friends with him, I would come to realize that although maybe not to the same extremes as this night, this wasn't far off from being a typical open bar for him. The phrase, "Open bar, dude" sadly is one I've become very familiar with. I have been DD again since this night, but if he is coming along, I always insist on driving his truck. This relieves me of the responsibility of clean up for future incidents in the backseat. I can still smell it every time I think about it.

One thing this whole experience taught me is a bit of self-control. I have had more than my fair share once or twice now, but at some point, I know in the back of my head that I need to slow down a bit before I go "full Jeremy." I still love going to the Christmas parties and thankfully many years have passed since this occurred, so it has faded into memory a bit and my wife hasn't had to push kick any of my co-workers since then.

Dorothy

Apple martinis? What was I thinking? This is one of only two times in my entire life that I genuinely considered never drinking again. I make the active decision to forget this night ever happened due to the headache and hangover that followed the following morning.

Also, I still own those boots and yes, they are as awesome as I say.

Jeremy

"Open bar, dude."

GET IN THE BACK

John

At some point in everyone's life, they will screw up in such a way, that each time they think about it, a chill will run down their spine as they shudder while recalling the embarrassment they experienced. This story is about such a day in my life. A day where my decision-making resulted in such a colossal shit of the bed, that it would shatter my confidence in nearly every aspect of my life for a long time to come.

I had been on the fire department for a little less than a year, so I was still pretty new, to say the least. Each firefighter on our department goes through a probationary period of 6 months after you complete about 5 months of training. During the training period and probationary period after, you are given a bright yellow helmet to wear. This basically helps more senior individuals keep an eye on you by purposefully making you stick out like a sore thumb. At the time this story took place, I had only recently finished my probationary period and earned my black helmet, which means two things. First, since my department was a hybrid volunteer department, they had people not only respond from home, but they also had 12-hour day and night shifts you could sign up for since you were no longer a yellow helmet. Second, you still don't know shit and have a long way to go because you haven't seen anything yet.

Keeping this in mind, my recently awarded black helmet and I were working one of our first shifts. I was excited since this was my first time working out of station 1 headquarters, which always gets the most calls. We had two paramedics working on the ambulance and the engine crew consisted of 4 more people including me. The paramedics were from a 3rd party service and didn't interact with us too much. The other firefighters I was working with were 2 very seasoned guys, Mark and Mike, who had 30 years of experience between them, along with another firefighter named Randy who had been on the department for about 5 years.

Mike was our lieutenant, and he is one of the nicest guys I have ever met to this day. He always went out of his way to help others and teach guys like me the ropes. I recall times where he would go above and beyond to show me things no one else would take the time to do. He was the reason I felt confident in my abilities when on an active scene. It was always a good feeling knowing he was going to be your officer for the shift.

Randy was older but you would have never guessed it from the level of energy he carried with him. His enthusiasm was always contagious. Mark was the engineer, which is the guy who drives and operates the pumps on the trucks. It's actually more difficult than I make it sound.

As a stark contradiction to the other two guys on the shift, Mark is by far one of the grumpiest and rudest people I have ever met. I mostly remembered him from my training classes that he taught when he took pleasure in intimidating people that knew less than him.

My shift started at 6pm, but I got there around 5pm to get a head start on chores and make a good impression. As the newer guy who hadn't really worked many shifts and hadn't proven himself yet, leaving a good impression is always a good idea. The more senior guys tend to notice people who go the extra mile and if you do it for them, they will usually return the favor. Firefighting involves building relationships and trust, so this is part of the gig when you're the new guy.

The shift started simply and routine enough. I did a ton of chores and made sure all our equipment was working properly. Every now and then, the tones would go off for a routine medical call. Around 9pm, the tones went off again, but this time it was for a multi-vehicle accident. We got to the scene quickly. No one was majorly hurt, and the call went smoothly. Our crew was working like a well-oiled machine; efficient and effective. I even managed as the new guy to get a rare bit of praise from Mark as he told me I, "did good" on the call.

We didn't end up getting back to the station until about 10:30pm and after taking a few minutes to defuse, everyone started getting ready to get some sleep for the night. By midnight, everyone had gone to bed except me. Sleeping on a shift was never easy for me. I was always on edge. I genuinely cared so much about doing a good job, that I actively avoided anything that could even slightly jeopardize my performance. The idea of lying in a nice comfortable bed always made me worry that I would sleep through the tones somehow, so I always ended up being the guy who would just stay up and eventually fall asleep on the couch in the common room watching T.V.

Dooooooooo do do do do dooooo...........

The tones were going off, waking me from my slumber on the couch as I scrambled up trying to figure what time it was. I rubbed my eyes, squinting to focus on the clock. 2am. Got it. It was a Friday night, and that probably meant a drunk driver going home caused an accident. I started heading towards my gear rack before the dispatcher even said what was happening. The doors from the bunk rooms began opening as everyone else slowly emerged, most of them yawning, still putting shirts or pants on while half asleep as they made their way to the gear racks too. Just as I was just about to put my bunker gear on, the call came through and much to everyone's surprise, it was not a car accident. It was far worse.

"Attention Station 1, report to...." the dispatcher's voice began over the intercom system. They then gave the address followed by, "for an active shooting in progress with multiple victims." It made my stomach sink and my heart shoot up into my throat. This was going to be an intense and completely new experience for me. You get a lot of training on fire departments, but oftentimes you will encounter calls where training only gets you so far. The idea of responding to an active shooting scene on paper can be easily broken down into standard procedures to follow. Actually, responding to one in real life carries a lot more anxiety and pressure that a textbook will never be able to properly capture.

I turned to look back towards everyone else and they now had much more pep in their step. I did the same, quickly putting on my gear and hopping into the back of the firetruck. I took a quick moment to center myself and run through all the protocols for a call like this. I knew as an EMT Basic, I was only to do as I was told by paramedics. I needed to be sure I was doing all the grunt work required to make sure they had everything they needed. I did a quick visual exercise in my head, running through where everything I needed was, and made my plan of attack for how I would give the most support possible.

As everyone else hopped on the engine, the ambulance was already taking off, but a volunteer responder had just pulled in looking to go with. I noticed it was one of the new guys named Christian. He was still a probationary, but he was already an EMT Basic too, so he would be especially useful for this call. He quickly grabbed his gear and got in the back with Randy and me, then off we went.

"Attention all responders," dispatch came back over the radio. "The scene is no longer active. You are now clear per command to enter the incident area."

What a relief, I thought to myself.

Don't get me wrong, I knew what I was signing up for when I became a firefighter, but that doesn't make those realities any easier to confront. It can be a bit of a contradiction sometimes. Most people go into the fire service because they want to help others, but these types of calls can make you feel a bit helpless sometimes.

We arrived at the scene within minutes. It wasn't hard to spot the incident since there were roughly 20 police vehicles already surrounding the home where everything had taken place. We got off the truck and I took a split second to look around me at all the chaos. The night was illuminated by red and blue lights flashing everywhere, occasionally shining on some of the bodies that were scattered throughout the yard or on the street. Police officers were still scrambling around everywhere going in and out of the house with evidence kits while others were putting up the yellow crime scene tape, blocking the scene off from the public. A few more officers could be found dotted around the edges of the incident, sitting next to the people who were still living, trying to comfort them after their gruesome experience.

The night had probably begun so different for these people. They came to a nice house party to be with friends and then something like this happened. It seemed that tempers must have flared between some of the guests and one person pulled a firearm. It was a senseless tragedy.

Over the radio, you could hear that more ambulances were responding from stations 2 and 3 of our department. We had 2 dead-on-arrival, multiple people with severe but not life-threatening injuries, 5 more critically wounded, and 2 walking wounded.

I went to work quickly, springing to action the plan that I had outlined in my head earlier. I grabbed equipment from each vehicle and provided any assistance I could to the paramedics who were hard at work. Thankfully, Mike & Randy were also experienced paramedics, so they were pulled off our engine to assist the ambulance crews. Our backup arrived quickly as everyone continued to work. It was a controlled chaos with people running to help where needed depending on who was more critical. Despite the chaotic nature of the scene, everyone did their job and after about 20 minutes, all patients were given pre-hospital care and loaded into different ambulances for transport to the nearest hospital. We had done everything we could.

As I watched each ambulance head down the street, out of view, I realized something truly terrifying. I scanned through the sea of police and firefighters remaining on the scene, desperately trying to confirm my suspicion. I first saw Mark, still standing by the firetruck, arms crossed looking as chipper as ever. Then I spotted Christian, talking with one of the officers before turning and beginning to walk back to the truck as well. No Randy. No Mike. We would be operating with a skeleton crew until they could return from the hospital, but this realization came with the now confirmed, horrifying reality that I was suddenly senior on the truck. Although Mark was technically way more experienced, he was the engineer, making me the officer in place of Mike.

My eyes darted side to side, wide as could be, still searching around for some sort of hope that either Mike or Randy magically stayed behind. There was no such hope.

"This can't be," I thought to myself. I had no clue how to be an officer. Firefighters aren't even able to become an officer without months of schooling and a minimum of 5 years on the department, yet somehow, I was going to be the officer for what could be the remainder of the shift. There is an enormous responsibility that comes with this. I would be the leader for the entire crew if we got another call like this. If there was a fire, I would be required to radio in detailed information, referred to as a size up, for all other responding units. They would prepare based on my directions. I would be determining action methods for approaching a fire scene. People's lives would rest on my decision-making.

The pressure was on and I could feel it. I nervously walked up to Mark, who understandably didn't seem like he was in the best of moods, and asked him plainly, "Should I really take officer's seat?" He immediately let out a loud single, "HA" which didn't exactly boost my confidence any.

"I guess we don't have a choice. Just don't break anything and pretend like you actually know what you're doing."

I rolled my eyes at him to pretend like his words didn't bother me, but he unknowingly struck fear into me by giving me the realization that I could potentially break something. It was one more thing that I didn't really want to worry about. I had enough on my mind.

I walked around the front of the truck and over to the officer's door, which is the front passenger side door, opened it up, and climbed up the first few steps that lead to the seat. It is a fairly spacious area, all black, with several switches above your head and on the dashboard in front of you. There is also a large, elevated center counsel, which contains more buttons, along with the radio and a few other things I didn't know what to do with. I cannot understate how intimidated I was. I actually had to take a moment to tell myself I could do this before hopping the rest of the way in. I knew I needed to be ready in case another call came through. I could do this!

Just as I was stepping in, I saw Mike's bunker gear was still sitting on the seat. Since he didn't need it on the ambulance, we would just take it back to the station and put it away for him. I moved the gear down onto the floor space in front of me and sat down in the seat, pulling the door closed behind me. I was distracted with a million thoughts running through my head including rehearsing exactly what I was about to say as I made my first ever, "returning to station" call over the radio as an officer.

RRRROOOOOOOOOOOOOOEEEEEEEEEEE
EEEEEEEEEEEEEEEEEEEEEEEEEEEEEEEEEEEEE
EEEEEEEEEEEEEEEEEEEE..........

What the hell is happening? What is that? Who is doing this? Wait it's us!

The fire siren started going off out of nowhere. Just to be clear, this wasn't the quieter wee-woo siren either. It was the loud as all hell, deafening truck siren blasting at full pitch and was so loud that I couldn't think clearly due to the amount of panic it was inducing. For a moment, I covered my ears. There was a good reason for why we normally wore ear protection when that siren was being used.

So here we were, in the middle of a neighborhood, on an active crime scene at 3am with our truck siren screaming endlessly into the night. If the residents of the surrounding homes weren't awake from all the commotion before, they were now. I looked out the front window of the truck to see most of the police either covering their ears too or desperately waving at us to stop. Some of them were so on edge that their hands had moved to their sidearms, maybe assuming this was a call for help.

My first time as an officer on the fire engine was not off to a good start, to say the least as cops started pouring out of the house to see what was going on. I looked over to the driver's seat to find Mark, who fumbled his way into the truck as quickly as he could. His normal pissed-off grumpy face had been replaced by sheer wide-eyed panic as he looked up at me with his hands waving frantically through the air. His lips were moving rapidly underneath that stupid grumpy man mustache of his, and I'm sure he was yelling at me, but I couldn't hear a thing over the blaring siren.

I uncovered my ears finally allowing his voice to break through the noise. "You're on the key, dumbass!"

This meant nothing to me. What's a key? The only keys I knew of were right there in the ignition. So, I did the only logical thing and pointed my fingers at the keys. "Now who's the dumbass, Mark. What kind of engineer can't even find the keys in the one place they are supposed to be?" I thought to myself. "What is wrong with you? How stupid are you?" he replied.

Damnit!" was all I could hear him say next. Clearly, he still thought this was my fault, so I quickly put my hands into the air to show I wasn't touching anything, most likely making the stupidest face possible.

"No, not your hands you moron! Your foot! Move your feet!" he yelled. I immediately picked my feet up off the ground and even grabbed the back of my knees to prove I wasn't doing anything while simultaneously looking like a complete jackass. At this point, I looked like I was giving birth in the front seat of a fire truck as everyone looked on. Amidst all the noise, panic, and confusion I stared out the window from between my legs at the many officers still approaching our vehicle or covering their ears, and the thought began to cross my mind that maybe I had indeed, actually broke something.

Mark batted his hand at me, dismissing my idiocy, and started flipping switches above his head on the dashboard. These must have been some sort of kill switches, but they were not working as the siren continued its ear-splitting sound, unphased by his stupid switches. I tried my best to do my part, sloshing from side to side looking for something or anything that resembled a button I could press. I didn't know what any of these buttons did, but maybe I would get lucky, right? After I completed my thorough panic search of my surroundings with no such success, I looked back down to my feet, picking them up and assuming the birthing position again, looking through the gap in my legs at the floorboard still trying to figure out whatever this key thing was. That's when it struck me.

Mike's gear!

I moved his equipment that I had set down earlier to look underneath it. There it was! A little pedal-like object built into the floor. This has to be what Mark was talking about. I found the key!

Why is it called a key? What a dumb name for this device. It is a floor pedal or siren pedal at best. Fire departments tend to get obsessed with these stupid technical names for things rather than just calling it was it is.

Regardless, I shoved the gear off the key and over to the other side of the floorboard.

EEEEEEEEEEEEEEEEeeeeeeeeerrrrrrrrrrrrrro ooooo. The siren began coming to a slow, painful stop. While it wound down it made little blips of different pitches, almost like it was coughing and tired from having been blasted at full pitch for so long. Finally, it came to a complete stop and I was met with silence at last.

My ears were still ringing as I looked up and the fear started to set in, realizing what I had done. All my hard work, showing up to shift early, doing extra chores, trying to make a good impression, had all been undone, possibly forever.

I looked out the front window and there were several officers still cautiously moving towards the truck, each of them looking just as pissed off as Mark does on a normal day. They were either trying to see if everything was okay, or a more likely scenario, they were discussing who got the pleasure of killing the person responsible. Namely, me. I knew what was coming next, but I couldn't bring myself to willingly confront it. I just wanted to crawl into a ball and wake up from this awful nightmare.

"HEY!" Mark yelled at me from the driver's seat.

I shuddered, slowly turning my head to look at him. I was giving him the look that acknowledged how badly I screwed up, hoping for mercy.

"Get in the fucking back." He said sternly, expressing complete disgust directed at me in a way I had personally never experienced before.

I turned away from Mark, head down and tail between my legs as I opened the door and hopped down out of the officer's seat. I heard Mark behind me continuing to mumble something I'm sure was directed at me. I kept my eyes on the ground, doing my own little walk of shame to the back door, only looking up once to see an officer shaking his head at me and a family who had probably been woken by me that came out on their front lawn wondering what was going on. I opened the back door, and quickly jumped into the nearest seat, shutting the door behind me. I had never been so embarrassed and ashamed in my entire life. As I got settled in, I looked up and across from me to find Christian, the probationary, sitting there, lips pursed and eyes wide, looking at me to acknowledge that I definitely just screwed up big time. Noticing him startled me just a bit. I was so focused on all the embarrassment and shame, I had honestly forgotten he was still there, witnessing everything happen from the backseat.

"I didn't......I didn't know the thing was on the ground," I said.

"Yeah, I could tell," he replied simply. Thanks, Christian.... way to be supportive.

"Engine 1 is out of service, returning to station," Mark said over the radio from the front.

"10-4, Engine 1," dispatch replied. A probationary firefighter cannot ride in the officer's seat, removing the possibility of Christian filling my inadequate shoes, so rather than continue with me as officer, Mark actually opted to go back to the station and take our crew out of service for the time being. I don't necessarily disagree with his choice, given my initial performance.

We drove back to the station in complete and total silence. No one said a word. As we pulled back into the station, I'm not even sure I waited until the truck had been turned off to jump out, which is against the rules, but I might as well stay par for the course on this kind of night. I took off my gear quickly before either of the others could even make it to the gear racks and booked it. The embarrassment and dread of the new asshole I was about to be ripped, sent me into panic mode. I made a B-line for the bathroom, which is where I considered staying for the rest of the shift, pretending that I was taking the biggest shit of my life. In reality, I was just going to sit there silently, contemplating how badly I truly screwed up and preparing myself for whatever punishment was coming my way. For how well my shift had started, I sure did find my way to rock bottom pretty quickly. I had never been so low.

Eventually, I couldn't take it anymore. I needed to just get it over with and face the music. I finally mustered up the courage to stick my head out of the bathroom and walk back into the common room, where I expected to have everyone sitting there waiting to completely destroy me. However, it was surprisingly quiet. It seems that everyone actually went back to sleep. As for me, not a chance. There would be no sleep. There would only be sitting, listening to the dull ringing still in my ears and watching the clock count down the minutes until 6am when my shift ended.

Oddly enough though, this boded really well for me. It was already 5am and the next shift started in an hour. It isn't uncommon when a shift had a mid-morning call like we did, that the crew will sleep in a bit. It isn't like anyone on the incoming shift needed the bunk room since they worked during the day. I may have gotten very lucky, and I could escape, delaying my punishment for another day.

Unfortunately, it wasn't meant to be. At about 5:45am, I ventured out of the common room as the next shift walked in and I spotted Mark talking to them. Damn him for waking up early. I attempted to slither along the walls, staying out of sight while making my way slowly to my gear rack to gather all of my things and high tail it out of there. However, I watched as Mark stopped talking to the other guys mid-sentence. He stuck his nose in the air, almost like he could smell my fear, giving away my position. He turned my way and spotted me immediately.

"Hey, dumbass! Where do you think you're going? Get over here! Now!" I walked over, completely defeated. There was no getting away now. Once I made it to him, he thoroughly ripped me a new one in front of everyone. I knew that this was coming, but I didn't quite expect it to be this much of a spectacle. Mark yelled at me until he was basically out of breath. I hardly caught any of what he said, only bits and pieces, mostly involving name-calling. It sucked. Everyone just stood there and watched. I decided it was best to just stare at the floor until he was finished with his relentless barrage of insults.

Word of my siren blunder spread through the rest of the department like wildfire. I felt like I would never hear the end of it. However, there is something truly beautiful about being on a fire department. It is always just a matter of time until someone else screws up just as bad or worse than you did. Then, everyone's attention turns elsewhere, and you can finally return to some sort of normalcy. Then you carry on, doing your best while praying that you never screw up like that ever again. But you will.......... you will.

Reflection

It took me a long, long time before I ever told anyone outside of the department about this story. Embarrassment doesn't actually sum up everything I felt that night. I'm not actually sure there is a word in the dictionary that can properly capture all of the emotions I felt when this happened. I took pride in being a capable firefighter and this was not representative of my normal performance. It was a real hit to the ego.

Eventually, I saw it for what it was, a giant hilarious mistake. I got in over my head and I paid for it. Experiencing this just reinforced how crazy things can get and although Firefighting is a pretty serious job, there can be plenty of humor that comes from it too. Even if it was only funny at your expense.

I never once sat in the officer's seat ever again. In fact, I avoided it at all costs, instead, leaving that job to those far more capable than myself. All it took was one experience to make me realize how little I knew and how unprepared I was. I never wanted to feel that bad about something ever again.

Contrary to that, however, I did gain something from this experience. I gained a level of respect for the men and women that sit on those officer seats that I never had before. By all means, I respected it before, but going through this made me realize how much responsibility they are burdened with during a call. They are incredibly capable people whose judgement and decision-making are above and beyond most others. My hat goes off to them.

I am no longer a firefighter, but during the remainder of my time with the department, I never once signed up for another shift out of station 1. Of course, Mark never let me live that down and was actively a jerk to me on most days. People always told me it was just Mark being Mark, but he just made it feel so personal. Either way, I don't hold any grudges anymore and I wish him the best despite him being a total dick.

I think after everything was said and done, I was a pretty good firefighter, and I am happy for every single moment, both good and bad, that it gave me.

I GOT IN A FIGHT WITH AN ALIEN

<u>Walt</u>

The invention of Wikipedia really set me back. I have always been the type of person that enjoys going down an informational rabbit hole. But before the internet and Wikipedia, there were books. Remember those? I'm an avid reader of all genres, but I genuinely enjoy reading books that come in a series. Why stop at one? I have read anything from war novels to biographies, and everything in between. However, one particular phase of reading stands out the most.

I was in my early 20's and had a job working at a nuclear plant. It was the 1980's and I was recently out of the army, trying to settle back into real life again. I held the position of Fuel Handler, which basically means I was one of the people responsible for offloading and reloading nuclear fuel out of and back into the reactor core. The job also comes with a million other tasks too long to list. I genuinely enjoyed my job and I continued to work there until the day I retired. However, there is one part of the job, called an outage, that is a bit less enjoyable, and anyone who works at a nuclear plant will probably agree. An outage is where the plant shuts down the generating units or other equipment to do scheduled maintenance. Most likely, we'd be refueling the station to continue generating power. This means long shifts and 7-day work weeks. At the time this event took place, we were currently in an outage. However, the one upside to being a fuel handler during an outage is the large amount of downtime in between assigned tasks, which means more time for me to read.

I had recently gotten very into alien abduction books. First, I started off by reading all about the "science" behind them, like how all the different accounts are so eerily similar to one another, despite never having had contact with one another. People could even describe devices that were used on them in different parts of the world speaking different languages. Many of these books would even get into the statistics that could determine the likelihood of abduction based on where you live. All the fun stuff, you know?

More recently though, I had gotten into firsthand accounts of people who claimed to have been abducted themselves. It was absolutely fascinating to read about the things people said happened to them. The detail that they remembered was what stuck out to me the most. I remember also thinking, what was in it for them? I always approach most things in life from a skeptical point of view. Figuring out if a person could gain from telling a story or if they could have ulterior motives is one of the litmus tests I perform on any story. However, while claiming that you were kidnapped by creatures from another planet, who then took you to their ship and did unthinkable things to you may be one way to get attention, it isn't the type of attention that a lot of people want. In fact, many of the people featured in the books were reputable people such as high-ranking military figures, doctors, or other people from typically respectable positions in our society. What I'm essentially getting at is that they have a lot to lose and not a lot to gain. So, for them to go out and tell their story, in my mind, gave them a little bit of legitimacy.

Each time I was working I would read more and more, diving deeper into the details of the experiences of these individuals. I would often forget where I was as my interest in the stories would pull me in, until a co-worker might come up and startle me by tapping me on the shoulder, letting me know there was work to be done.

When an outage occurs at a plant, the fuel handler division that I was a part of is separated into two different groups. The handling crew and the lubrication crew. In this instance, I was part of the lubrication crew, which meant I had to ensure that all equipment was properly maintained. This included oil changes and lubricating huge machinery that operated both on and off the plant premises.

To make this outage suck a little more than most, I also got stuck working the night shift, which was a 6 p.m. to 6 a.m. time slot. One small upside to third shift is it has fewer regular duties by comparison to the day shift, which meant even more reading time than a usual outage.

Each night of work went by the same way. I sat there going through each page of my book, reading about people being pulled into ships to be poked and prodded. There were some nights with so little to do, that I would read nearly an entire book during the shift. Until one night, we got the call to do a job I hated more than most.

Any nuclear plant is near a water source such as a river, lake, or ocean because that water source is pumped into different plant systems to act as a cooling agent to regulate temperatures on different components. This also means that somewhere nearby there will be buildings that hold the gigantic water pumps. My job that night was to change the oil on one of the larger pumps in the fleet. To give a bit of perspective, the engine on your typical vehicle is around 1.5 gallons. The oil reservoir on this pump is a little more than one hundred gallons. Just to sweeten the deal, the location of the reservoir that required changing was located underground. This means I'd be climbing down through a tiny hole in the floor and working in confined spaces. It was all my least favorite jobs rolled into a nice little unpleasant bundle.

My partner for this task, Duncan, and I loaded up the truck and got ready to go. Duncan was an older guy, short and round, with combed-back long gray hair that was thinning on top, and a long gray beard to match. He always wore an expression on his face that indicated he was displeased with everything around him. To top it off, since he had already been around for so long, he let the younger guys like myself do most of the work while he just sat there telling us how he would do it better. Can you tell how excited I was?

After the truck was loaded, we headed out to the pump station, which was about a 10-minute drive. Duncan took the initiative to drive, but don't let that deceive you, because when we got to the fence that secured the pump station, it meant he wouldn't have to get out and undo all the chains and locks on the gate to open everything up.

We pulled up to the fence around 3 a.m. I got out to start undoing the several chains and padlocks that kept the area secure from the public. The building was about 500 yards from the road, but at this time of year, it was barely visible since it sat at the edge of a tall cornfield near the river. Also, instead of a road leading to the station, there was just a section of short grass, wide enough for 2 vehicles to fit side by side. On either side of the short grass road leading to the building were corn stalks about 6 feet tall. There were a few light posts on each side, that glowed a faint dull yellow as they led towards the building.

I got back in the truck and we drove along the bumpy path leading to the station and as we got closer, it came into full view. I had been to this station before, but never at night. The atmosphere was eerie, to say the least. During the day, the building itself wasn't too out of the ordinary. It was just a large windowless metal building, standing about 40 feet tall with 7 or 8 steps leading to the single gray metal door that was the only entrance or exit. However, on a night like tonight, one that was pitch black due to cloud cover and the new moon, the building took on a much more sinister feeling. The kind that makes you feel on edge like you're waiting for something bad to happen at any moment. We came to a stop and I got out first. The ground was soft and damp from being so close to the river. I searched for my tools on the truck with a flashlight since the building only had a few dull yellow lights on the front above the main door and the still faint yellow glow of the light posts behind us did virtually nothing. The faint sound of the pump running inside the building created a low grumbling hum as it pumped water to the towers. On our right, past the tall corn was the river flowing with its heavy current. It smashed into the rocks, creating a thick mist that spread into the air dispersing what little light we had.

All those alien books I had been reading were allowing my mind to race just a little too much. If I were an alien and I wanted to abduct someone, this is where I would do it. Come to think of it, I would probably pick a guy just like me. You know, the guy who had recently become obsessed with abductions and when he went around afterward telling everyone it happened to him, they would be able to write it off easily by saying the books were getting to me. That it was all in my head. I was the perfect target and the aliens probably knew it. However, I just had to keep telling myself that the chances of being abducted were so low that I needed to stop worrying about it. Plus, I had Duncan with me, who had finally just gotten out of the truck and was walking about 30 feet behind me as I approached the stairs.

As I walked up the steps to the door, it was as if the mist got thicker, reducing visibility to only a few feet. I turned around and could barely see the bottom of the steps anymore, where Duncan was standing. Once at the door, I put the key in, but it was difficult to turn since everything, including me, was covered in a layer of moisture from the fog. As I wiggled the key while shaking the door a bit, finally getting it to turn, my feet nearly slipped out from under me. Seems the metal mixed with the constant mist made the platform and steps incredibly slippery too.

I turned back to Duncan, "Hey! Careful coming up the stairs. It's really sli...." I cut myself off mid-sentence. As I pulled the door open, I sensed something in front of me coming through the door. It was fast! Before I had time to react, it lunged at me to attack. I was caught completely off guard as it landed the first blow, punching me directly in the bridge of my nose. The pain caused me to squint, limiting my visibility even further. I tried to back up, but as my feet nearly slipped out from under me again, I quickly realized that doing so would send me falling down the metal staircase.

The attack continued relentlessly. I peered through my blurred vision, trying to discern exactly what was happening. I tried to make out the identity of the assailant, but it stayed right in my face, leaning its weight on me. I was able to push it off me and I heard its body smack against the metal wall of the building exterior, but before I could get a clearer look at it, it lunged back at me, hitting me in the face again. I could only make out that it was about six feet tall with long thin white hair.

"Oh no," I thought to myself. Everything slowed down and I began to hear my heart beating like it was about to burst out of my chest. I felt paralyzed as fear ran through my entire body. This was it. They had come for me. The aliens were here to abduct me, and I had nowhere to run. I quickly looked back again and didn't see Duncan standing at the bottom of the steps anymore. Maybe they got him too? I needed to do something before the ship came and beamed me up. I needed to fight! I'm a fairly well-built guy so I had a chance as long as it stayed one on one. So, I made up my mind right then and there, that I was not going to go down so easily.

I swung with my right hand and missed. The alien was too close to me for my punch to generate any power and I still couldn't back up without risking a nasty fall.

Thankfully, this wasn't the first fight I had been in during my life, so I adapted. After recovering my balance, I extended my left arm, grabbing the alien around its neck and putting a bit of distance between us. I stopped for a split second, shocked since I had never felt anything like this before. Its neck was hard and very skinny but covered with what felt like some sort of slime or greasy coating. It was disgusting. I kept a strong grip around its neck, reared back, and began punching the alien in the face repeatedly. I kept telling myself that today was not the day I'm getting abducted. With its hair swinging around wildly, I yelled in a war cry-like fashion while I relentlessly continued my counterattack.

After several more direct blows, I felt the alien go limp and I knew it was time to finish the fight. I grabbed it around the neck with both hands now, took a slight sidestep, and...

"EEEEEEEEEEEYYYAAAAAAAHHHHHHH!" I screamed, letting it know I meant business, as I put every bit of force I had into throwing the skinny necked son of a bitch down the stairs behind me. The alien went tumbling down, end over end, disappearing through the mist to the bottom of the stairs and I knew victory was mine. There was no coming back from that. It was just going to have to run or float or do whatever its stupid alien ass does back to its ship.

I remember thinking to myself that I should reach out to one of the authors of the books I've read. My story would be sure to blow all the others out of the water. I have never read about people fighting back and winning before. They picked the wrong guy to try and mess with this time.

I took a few cautious steps down, exhausted, breathing heavily, looking on as the alien laid at the bottom of the steps, lifeless, but something still wasn't right. I heard something over to my left and I looked over to find Duncan, rolling around on the ground, laughing hysterically. I couldn't understand why he would be laughing at a time like this. Maybe the sight of real aliens made him lose his mind? It didn't make sense.

The fog was thicker than ever. Less light than even before helped me make out anything as I looked again towards the alien at the bottom of the steps. It continued to lay there, unconscious, possibly dead. I wiped the mist from my face and eyes to get a clearer picture of my attacker from another planet as I slowly approached the body. I walked down the final few steps, standing over my alien assailant, studying its body up close. The problem is that most people would not refer to it as an alien. Most people would refer to it by its more common name. A mop.

That's right. A mop. I beat the shit out of a mop. As it would turn out, the skinny neck I grabbed was merely the broom handle and the long white hair was the mop end. Apparently, some of the other operators are very aware of how creepy this building is at night and they like to play jokes on one another, such as propping a mop up on the other side of the door, so that when opened, it will fall on you and scare the shit out of you. What they didn't expect was for an alien obsessed fuel handler to find the mop first and unintentionally scar him for life. Worse yet, after Duncan finished up laughing, which took a very long time, I knew that two things were going to happen. First, we still had to go crawl underground in a confined space where I would not be able to escape his ridicule while changing a one-hundred-gallon oil tank. Second, was when we returned to the power plant, Duncan would be sure to tell anyone willing to listen that I beat the living hell out of a mop at a pumping station.

The rest of the night went as one might expect. While in close quarters with Duncan, working on the pump, I could still hear his occasional chuckling over the loud humming of the station equipment. Once we got back to the main plant, my prediction came true. He walked off and told everyone about my valiant effort to save him from the evil mop that attacked us.

For weeks, I had to defend myself and tell them that after it hit me in the face, I just reacted and that they would probably do the same thing. They didn't buy it. I never once dared to tell anyone that because I had been reading alien books, I thought E.T. himself was attacking me. I'm not sure if any amount of time could have passed to be able to live that version of the story down. Nowadays, as I'm well into my retirement, I don't care about what people think, and I can finally tell the truth.

I got in a fight with an alien.

Reflection

As I look back on this now, one thing always comes to mind. I wish I would have taken more time while I was working to enjoy what I was doing and relish moments like these. Working at a power plant, especially a nuclear one, can be pretty serious business, and just like any job, it came with a lot of difficulty or inconveniences that I spent far too much time focused on. Everyone was always mad that we had to do this or that, and it really chipped away at how cool the jobs we were doing actually were. This story is a perfect example of that. I was annoyed that I had to change the oil on this particular pump, but in reality, not many people can say they changed a one-hundred-gallon, underground tank on a pump that cools nuclear fuel. It was a pretty cool job and I'm happy I got to do it for nearly 40 years, even if I had to deal with the occasional alien attacker.

As time has passed, I've done a 180 on how I feel about this story. I used to be so embarrassed that I beat up a mop, thinking I was being attacked by a scraggly-haired, skinny-necked extraterrestrial. I am not so easily embarrassed anymore, and I think of it as just a funny story that my family sometimes goads me into telling people who haven't heard it before. All in all, I get a kick out of it now.

Every time I tell the story I always remember how genuinely afraid I was that I was about to be abducted and probed. It's still very possible I never really recovered from this experience. I can say for certain that I go through doors more cautiously than I ever did before and I can also confirm that I never took the night shift during outages ever again. I still maintained my obsessive reading habits, but after this, I decided to stay away from the ghost or alien stuff. For now.